MONASTIC WISDOM SERIES: NUMBER TWENTY-THREE

Dieudonné Dufrasne, OSB

Dom Anselme Le Bail

Abbot of Scourmont 1913–1956

A monk, an abbot, a community

MONASTIC WISDOM SERIES

Patrick Hart, OCSO, General Editor

MW1 Cassian and the Fathers: Initiation into the Monastic Tradition
Thomas Merton, OCSO

MW2 Secret of the Heart: Spiritual Being
Jean-Marie Howe, OCSO

MW3 Inside the Psalms: Reflections for Novices
Maureen F. McCabe, OCSO

MW4 Thomas Merton: Prophet of Renewal
John Eudes Bamberger, OCSO

MW5 Centered on Christ: A Guide to Monastic Profession
Augustine Roberts, OCSO

MW6 Passing from Self to God: A Cistercian Retreat
Robert Thomas, OCSO

MW7 Dom Gabriel Sortais: An Amazing Abbot in Turbulent Times
Guy Oury, OSB

MW8 A Monastic Vision for the 21st Century: Where Do We Go from Here?
Patrick Hart, OCSO, editor

MW9 Pre-Benedictine Monasticism: Initiation into the Monastic Tradition 2
Thomas Merton, OCSO

MW10 Charles Dumont Monk-Poet: A Spiritual Biography
Elizabeth Connor, OCSO

MW11 The Way of Humility
André Louf, OCSO

MW12 Four Ways of Holiness for the Universal Church:
Drawn from the Monastic Tradition
Francis Kline, OCSO

MW13 An Introduction to Christian Mysticism:
Initiation into the Monastic Tradition 3
Thomas Merton, OCSO

MW14 God Alone: A Spiritual Biography of Blessed Rafael Arnáiz Barón
Gonzalo Maria Fernández, OCSO

MW15 Singing for the Kingdom: The Last of the Homilies
Matthew Kelty, OCSO

MW16 Partnership with Christ
Eugene Boylan, OCSO

MW17 Survival or Prophecy?
The Correspondence of Jean Leclercq and Thomas Merton
Patrick Hart, OCSO, editor

MW18 Light for My Path: Spiritual Accompaniment
Bernardo Olivera, OCSO

MW19 The Rule of Saint Benedict: Initiation into the Monastic Tradition 4
Thomas Merton, OCSO

MW20 Inside the School of Charity: Lessons from the Monastery
Trisha Day

MW21 Words for the Journey: A Monastic Vocabulary
Edith Scholl, OCSO

MW22 Come and See: The Monastic Way for Today
Brendan Freeman, OCSO

MONASTIC WISDOM SERIES: NUMBER TWENTY-THREE

Dom Anselme Le Bail

Abbot of Scourmont 1913–1956

A monk, an abbot, a community

by

Dieudonné Dufrasne, OSB

Saint-André de Clerlande Abbey

Preface by

Charles Dumont, monk of Scourmont

Epilogue by

Dom Armand Veilleux, abbot of Scourmont

Translated by

Elizabeth Connor, OCSO

Cistercian Publications

www.cistercianpublications.org

LITURGICAL PRESS

Collegeville, Minnesota

www.litpress.org

A Cistercian Publications title published by Liturgical Press

Cistercian Publications
Editorial Offices
Abbey of Gethsemani
3642 Monks Road
Trappist, Kentucky 40051
www.cistercianpublications.org

1 2 3 4 5 6 7 8 9

Library of Congress Cataloging-in-Publication Data

Dufrasne, Dieudonné.
Dom Anselme Le Bail, Abbot of Scourmont, 1913–1956 : a monk, an abbot, a community / by Dieudonné Dufrasne ; preface by Charles Dumont ; postface by Dom Armand Veilleux.
p. cm. — (Monastic wisdom series ; no. 23)
Includes bibliographical references.
ISBN 978-0-87907-023-6
1. Le Bail, Anselme, 1878–1956. 2. Abbots—Belgium—Chimay—Biography. 3. Trappists—Belgium—Chimay—Biography. 4. Monastic and religious life—Chimay—Biography. 5. Scourmont (Abbey : Chimay, Belgium) 6. Chimay (Belgium)—Church history. I. Title.

BX4705.L4225D84 2010
271'.12502—dc22
[B]

2009034784

Table of Contents

Preface

Those who knew him, his monks especially, will find him again with affectionate gratitude in these pages. Those who did not know him, will be able in these "approaches" to imagine him with his original and warm personality. Both of these types of readers will find with surprise and admiration a monk and man who knew how to integrate a healthy type of humanism into the concrete ideal of religious life.

Father Dieudonné has read, listened to, and let speak the young man, the young monk and then the Cistercian abbot. He has skillfully let us, in turn, listen to him and understand the joys and sufferings of a life totally given to God and his brothers.

Very conscious of the grace he had received along with his abbatial responsibility, Dom Anselme knew that he was the father of the community. He wanted to be, and said that he was. The motto he chose, "Abba Pater," and the divine Filiation of Christ which his coat of arms evoked, were meant to signify the sacramental task he was convinced he was fulfilling in this place and for his time.

One could say that he "made his time," giving a double sense to the word: he marked his time in his monastery and in the Order, but he also transmitted to others, by his teaching and the formation which he instilled, the task of perpetuating his work. If we take an overall view of these fifty-odd years of history, we cannot but be surprised before the unity and continuity of the community which he succeeded in keeping together in spite of two wars and the evolution of ideas and customs.

Father Thomas Merton, who from far-off Kentucky had sought to correspond with Dom Anselme, recognized—as Father

Dieudonné has pointed out—that he had prepared his community to live through these times of trial. Because he governed and formed the community of his monks in and by the community life which he lived with them, they do not have many personal remembrances. Here I can only mention a few—since I have been asked to do so—but I would like these several incidents to suffice to illustrate his way.

My first remembrance dates from February, 1942. The Germans were driving us out, and we had to move the library. We were exhausted with fatigue, it was cold, and I was a young novice. I met my abbot's glance. In that time of trial it was a look of connivance which I could not forget. We recognized this same look of effective and cordial sharing during our years of exile, when we would meet him in what he called "the gloomy crossroad," which was a mere caricature of a cloister.

In 1946, after our return from Momignies, at the time when there was question of my making a definitive commitment, the abbot took me with him on an interior tour of the monastery and asked me if I was ready to make profession. To my reply, if not evasive, at least not very enthusiastic—my health was already precarious—, he told me that in any case I must do what I loved. It was the first time that I had been advised to do what I loved, but that was surely what made me decide to commit myself and stay.

Among other *fioretti*: one day when he was walking past the desks in the study room, on mine he noticed a notebook of quotations. I had written on the cover: "*Plus eligere quam legere.*" "Select rather than read." Using sign language, he gently patted his hand on his chest, meaning that this was good. When I look at that notebook today, I feel that he is present and continuing to encourage me. Another time, he took me by surprise when I was scribbling some verses. He told me to continue, but moderately: this has helped me considerably ever since. He thought that the monk needed a hobby, something on the side which relaxes him.

I well remember the last time he looked at me. In his sad state of being unable to speak since his stroke, his eyes were full of tears; it was the day I left Scourmont for Caldey.

These looks, which were a blend of intelligence and affection, were rare and brief; but in an austere and silent life they create authentic bonds: there are brothers only on condition that they have a father. This charity of his, the quality of which has been called exceptional, also knew how to be severe, precisely when there was question of charity. So it was that one day when I went to see him to complain about how the monk in charge of the wardrobe room where I worked ran things, he no doubt detected a little bitterness in my criticism. Very calmly, and as if regretfully, he blessed me and showed me the door. One does not easily forget such a lesson.

Although he gave a special place to study, he also knew that balance among the three Benedictine works—liturgy, prayerful contemplative interior activity and manual work—remained essential. The disastrous situation of our finances after the war and occupation made the regular life difficult. Dom Anselme had the wisdom to emphasize work that would produce profit and to put several competent brothers in charge of it. He supported them by his confidence and let them run things and take the initiatives that were necessary. He entrusted the direction of work to Father Guerric who became his successor as abbot; and in spite of Father Theodore's reticence he put him in charge of the brewery.

Nevertheless, his attention to the community's spiritual culture which had been his principal preoccupation ever since he became abbot remained so. When speaking of a passage to read or some study that he wanted to share with the community—and in this way help them learn to read well—he often used Rabelais' expression: "essential marrow" (*moëlle substantifique*): one must go straight to what is essential and most nourishing. Would he perhaps like to have us listen to him reading this passage from the Prologue of *Pantagruel*, where Rabelais gave his instructions:

> One must open the book and carefully weigh what it means . . . You should be of good behavior, frequently studying and meditating, in order to whiff the scent of and to esteem these beautiful meaty books, to snap the bone and suck the essential (*substantifique*) marrow.

Was it not by phrases like these, written in a style that still had something of the Middle Ages about it and which he liked to recite like a troubadour, that he introduced us to the value of *lectio divina* which he was trying to restore in the Order?

To quote again from my notebook of texts, here is one that has always seemed to me to express the spiritual atmosphere familiar to us at Scourmont during the time of Dom Anselme. The quotation consists of several verses by Paul Claudel:

> And no one in this temple which is the world
> would ever be able to escape from the necessity of ample ceremony.
> Let them simply open their eyes to what they are doing and
> Let them consent to this mystery in which they are participating.
>
> (*La ville*, 2nd version, Act III)

In these few lines, which we could comment on at length, do we not find the ideal of a religious community? But the words "ample ceremony" remind me of a characteristic of Father Abbot, in the liturgy as well as in his whole life. There was something about him that was ample, in his bearing, his gests and his voice, as well as in his ideas, his projects and judgements. Such amplitude revealed greatness of spirit and a generous heart. Henri Bosco, in "*Le Mas Théotime*" spoke of "the benefits of amplitude which counterbalances the impetus of the soul and preserves its equilibrium. It is acquired only by recollection and unhurried concentration. . . . It is a large and calm view of the world, natural to people who live close to the earth." Dom Anselme, like every true monk, radiated peace, but a peace acquired at the price of "untiring work, frequent disappointment and a sentiment of true humility."

The pedagogy of Cistercian formation, which according to him ought to flow naturally from this peace, should therefore begin with what is interior and spread to what is exterior: the observances. These, instead of influencing the spiritual aspect automatically, should on the contrary emanate from it as by redundancy of the spirit on the body, heart and affectivity, and should be the place where they meet.

In his teaching and his way of governing he perseveringly maintained, in spite of criticism, this conviction about the primacy of what is spiritual and interior over regular observances. In his sermon for the profession of Father Maur and Father Francis, in 1937, one can read what he had already stated in his work: "*Cîteaux. La Trappe*," written in 1926. There he applied it to the liturgy, but for him liturgy was the expression of the whole of life: a continual liturgy.

Such an about-face, although it may seem evident today, was not so at that time and could get lost from sight. Everything that we can put under the term *lectio divina* is unified finally in what Saint Bernard calls *Consideration*, which is the heart of conversion and of the Cistercian life. It is *Consideration* which, "by purifying its own source, that is, the spirit which gives birth to it (I.8), orients our thoughts and action toward their sole ultimate end: contemplative union with God."

Among the circumstances which can change during the course of a lifetime and which formation will enable a person to live through as a monk, Dom Anselme mentioned illness: "The monk, confined to his bed for twenty-five years," he said in a sermon in 1937, "should remain a religious, prompt to will what God wills. That way he remains a religious perfectly: because his will is in accord with the spirit of the *Rule*, and in that way he practices it truly, to perfection." Was this not prophetic? Had he himself not religiously accepted the trial by which his life at Scourmont would end?

Even when he was an invalid unable to speak, for those who came in contact with him he still had this amplitude by which one could recognize him. This largess of his way of seeing things and of his spirit had its secret source in his fatherly heart. When Saint Bernard, in Book V of *On Consideration*, commented on the four "dimensions" of God according to Saint Paul's *Letter to the Ephesians*, he said that if God is "breadth" (3.18) it is because He is charity and charity is infinite and eternal (V.2).

After reading about this busy and unified life, what can we retain for ourselves except the fact that everything comes to an end, and that charity alone is endless (1 Co 13.4). With this same charity of which he left us such a beautiful memory, may Dom Anselme remember us and continue to love us.

Fr. Charles Dumont
Monk of Scourmont

Foreword

This work is not a biography in the academic sense of the word. For that reason we have deliberately chosen not to encumber the reader with an *apparatus criticus* which a university style historical work normally requires. In any case, the documentation which we have copiously consulted and quoted is found essentially in manuscripts available only in the archives of Scourmont Abbey. Consequently, if anyone wants to verify the authenticity of what we have written he or she should first obtain authorization to examine these archives, and especially should invest long hours of patient searching and laborious deciphering. We feel that we have done so honestly and with great care.

Since we do not wish to present arguments or prove anything, this work has no introduction, division into chapters or conclusion. In fact, when the monks of Scourmont asked me to undertake this work, we recognized that they had no desire to defend any thesis with regard to or based on a man—in this case Dom Anselme—, but rather that their only desire was to bring out the human and spiritual personality of a monk, a brother, an abbot—Dom Anselme—whose countenance remains astonishingly present today within these walls, and in the hearts of this community which he so loved: *amor loci et fratrum*.

As for me, writing this book was a unique experience, first of all because it is my first work of this type; secondly, and especially, because it was a marvelous experience. In fact, from day to day, though he is dead and we never knew him, this man, Father Abbot Dom Anselme Le Bail, seemed to be *"redivivus,"* living again. But was it the true Dom Anselme? Conversations with Scourmont monks who knew him, including sometimes long and moving talks with Father Charles Dumont, have left us with the assurance that the monk whose features we have drawn here from old rumpled pages was the real Dom Anselme.

We have therefore tried to discover this man by "approaches." This term expresses quite well the respect and modesty characteristic of this work. We have left out certain anecdotes which we heard, but which sometimes seemed too frivolous. We put aside in their folders notes which were too intimate. The years to come will erase them from their already yellowed pages. Neither of these two types of notes were necessary to either confirm or invalidate the material assembled in this book. A subjective piece of work? Yes, of course. The work of someone who, with all his heart, set out to meet another heart, large and fascinating: Dom Anselme Le Bail.

Dieudonné Dufrasne, OSB

If I tried to go further
If I longed for some place else, space
Illusion, dream or need?
That is all finished, my soul is weary.

Horizons are exalting,
I have so loved the sea, immensity
The happy departures one waits for,
Going higher, intense life.

Everything is a symbol and surpassed:
Sea, heights, immensity,
Everything takes on meaning and then disappears . . .
I reach reality.

C. D.

1

Remembrance of a fleeting moment

I am 16 at the time. He is 76. August 15, 1954. Between None and Vespers. The sky of the Assumption is radiant.

He is seated in a wheel chair. His pectoral cross stands out on his black scapular. His Swiss beret accentuates an intelligent forehead and determined eyebrows. His wheel chair is being pushed by a young monk all in white. I pass by him shyly, with the clumsy bashfulness of adolescents when they meet with handicapped old age.

He catches me with his vague regard, and nods to me with astonishing gentleness. After going further on, I turn around: the young monk is bending over close to the old man's ear. I imagine his tender words.

I continue on my walk across the open fields interspersed with birch and aspen trees: a landscape of fascinating breadth. France is just on the other side of the boundary posts. Here one runs up against earth of the foundations of the Ardennes, barren soil, with poor schist and spiny grass. It is summer: here, it comes quickly, but after a late spring that explodes in wild bundles of gorse. Still, there is some wind in the elms and other scattered trees. It is an unceasing wind, turning in circles. For centuries how many furnaces has it permitted to throb on streams such as the *Eau noire* or the *Wartoise*. The forges of another era fall in ruins amidst the silence of the copse, near hamlets which have names such as *Haut-Marais, Poteaupré, Forge Jean-Petit*.

I am on retreat at the Abbey of Forges-lez-Chimay, the Trappist monastery of Notre Dame de Saint Joseph at Scourmont, whose

Father Abbot is this paralyzed monk who has been unable to speak for five years. He would die on September 25, 1956, the day before I took the habit at the Benedictine monastery of Saint-André, at Loppen-les-Bruges. That day I had crossed the path of Dom Anselme Le Bail. An unforgettable moment in my memory.

Are you perhaps
More than three hundred leagues from here,
Or tossed into the sea
As food for the fish.

If you had preferred to stay
With your parents,
You would now be betrothed.

A Breton song

2

Who can guess his brother's horizon?

If I had been able or had dared that day to look deep into the eyes of this old man, I would no doubt have discovered horizons even more fascinating than those which had become dear to him since 1904, when he entered the novitiate at Scourmont. The young Emmanuel Le Bail, who became Brother Anselme when he was twenty-six years old, came from Brittany, from a hamlet located near the large town of Séglien, at Loc-Ouviern, in Morbihan. When someone has spent his youth between the impetuous Atlantic Ocean and the gentle woodlands of Lorien, later on he can not be other than a mixture of audacious tenacity and humble goodness. This may seem like a disconcerting mixture for whoever does not take the trouble to understand his brother's horizons.

He was born on December 31, 1878, the third child, following his sister Anne-Marie and his brother Joseph, and before Jerome who died at birth at the same time as his mother, Marie-Jeanne Leborgne, in 1880. Although he was deprived of a mother's irreplaceable tenderness he did not lack affection, especially from the old family servant Mary and his maternal aunt, Marie-Josèphe Leborgne.

In that setting one could every day feel the nearness of the Ocean with its large horizon. On the other hand, one had to accept the limits of living on the land of the family's farm, with its stables and two rooms with earthen floors. This constraint was diminished by the joy of passing long winter evenings in front of the immense hearth where a fire of huge—sometimes three feet long—logs burned, before closing himself into his typically Breton enclosed bed. It was no doubt there that little Emmanuel learned the bareness he would experience at La Trappe. Later on, Dom Anselme would like the austerity of the monastic life, but with humor that only those who have known "real" poverty are capable of.

3

When intelligence and piety embrace

When Emmanuel was eleven years old he left the primary school at Séglien to continue his studies first with the Lammenais Brothers at Pontivy, then at the Institute Saint-Jean-Baptiste at Guémené. Finally, from 1892 on, he began his Greek and Latin classical studies at the Minor Seminary of Sainte-Anne d'Auray.

In his archives Dom Anselme kept some precious traces of these six years of classical studies.

In his notebook from his last year there, where one can already discover the industrious handwriting that he kept right up until his death, quotations copied minutely from Greek and Latin authors follow one another; then Greek and Latin themes, and essays in French. From among these essays, here is one which he said was inspired by the *Legend of my big brother*:

> A monk built a cabin in the middle of a forest; he lived there all alone, his nourishment being the fruit of his work and the milk of two goats he possessed. He passed his life taking care of these animals and cultivating the land which he had cleared.
>
> One day, when he was coming back from pasture with his goats, he noticed that they were not as peaceful as usual. They ran along the path, leaping from one side to the other. Then they came back on the path and started butting each other and making all kinds of faces. They did this all the way to the stable. The monk was astonished; he tried to understand why they were doing it, but could not find any reason. It wasn't the weather, because it was the same as the days before. So he stopped thinking about it and went to bed, resolving to watch his goats attentively the next day.

> When he got up the next day he led his goats to the pasture as usual and guided them to the same place where they had been the day before. While he was attentively observing them he saw them nibbling the seeds of a bush. Then, after eating them, they ran around on the rocks and acted in the same capricious way as the day before. He tasted the seeds for himself, and found them a bit hard. When he returned home he made an extract from them and put it in boiling water. Suddenly, as he was stirring it, he became very nervous.
>
> So it was that coffee was discovered. . . .

Was he a brilliant student? He was too much of a dreamer and too whimsical to get very good marks: numerous letters he wrote to his father show this. And yet, he naively claimed to be the happiest man in the world. His passion : "I have caught madness about books," a madness he would not get over so quickly. At the beginning of his class in rhetoric he wrote in his notes that he had begun to get bored at home during vacation because he had no work to do: "Absolute leisure is something that is not suited to my nature." The rest of his life would bear that out very well! "I was next to him in the study hall," wrote one of his cousins, who became Fr. Guilloux, O.M.I.: "I never saw him break the rule of silence. He was serious and worked methodically. Already at that time he had adopted a habit of writing on file cards so as to have some order in his courses.

"Love of letters and desire for God": without guessing at his age that this formula would not escape stirring up controversy —he would realize it later!—, Emmanuel was a pious young boy. When he was 17 he consecrated himself to Mary:

> In the year of Our Lord 1895, in the month of March, after passing all the customary tests and giving full satisfaction, was admitted to our Congregation at the Minor Seminary of Auray, under the name of the Immaculate Conception, Monsieur Emmanuel Le Bail.

The next year, it was to the Holy Angels that he consecrated himself:

> Blessed Spirits, zealous defenders of God's glory and interests, tender and charitable friends of souls, I, Emmanuel Le Bail, in presence of the Immaculate Virgin Mary and all the saints, choose you as my patrons. I entrust to you the protection of my body and soul, all that I have and all that I am. To prove to you the sincerity of my devotion, with the help of grace I will strive to imitate your virtues, especially your humility, your obedience, your purity, your zeal for the glory of God, etc.

It was another epoch. Although Dom Anselme was ahead of his time, somewhere within him remained the trace of a man of this kind of piety, however interior and discreet, to the point that when he was abbot some people would reproach him for his lack of piety!

For centuries Sainte-Anne d'Auray had been, and remains, the principal shrine of pilgrimage in Brittany for afflicted people. "There is a fountain encircled with beautiful stone, with two joining pools. Inside the nave, the chapel was completely covered with large and small ex-votos, statues or images in wax and silver, crutches, aprons, clothing, prison shackles and other such things, which people brought from all parts of Brittany and even from Normandy, Mayne, Anjou and more distant provinces." (Dubuisson-Aubenay, 17e siècle). Emmanuel Le Bail frequently participated in the celebration of the "Great Pardon" in July, smiling and lost in the crowd of coifs and an abundance of cassocks.

Before an ambiguous and fragile light
Charms the horizon, one must love the night
Rather than trying to live, futile soul.

Repose in the bosom of the night to ripen your birth
Hope still again and dream a dream of unity,
At the end of our days we will take our distance.

Night of marriage with the Alone where is born the immensity
Of the earth and the heavens, of gods and mortals
Bursting forth of love like a splintered mirror.

C. D.

4

The combat of the young Jacob

Let us not be too quick to believe that because he had been "protected" by his healthy family atmosphere and the austerity of the Minor Seminary at Auray the young Emmanuel's religious vocation appeared to him by magic. No, on the contrary, it matured within the depths of real spiritual torment, and he finally reached his decision like a victory won over his interior demons. Here we recopy his personal notes, transcribing them literally in order to discover from his chaotic phrases the struggle he went through during the last year at the Minor Seminary.

> Always doubt and uncertainty. I contrive plans and ideas, and when everything is prepared for the best, I believe that it will never be anything but a dream. Because, in spite of all that, I see myself as being always attached to the world. While detesting it, I take pleasure in thinking about things of here below and I linger over the happiness and joys of this world. At other moments I am afraid that I am making a mistake and that one day I will regret that I cooked up such a plan. And aren't my fears well founded? Once I will have entered, it will be impossible to turn back, and I am afraid that I will fall under the burden. True, one must not lose hope in God's goodness, but I do not want to be presumptuous either. Oh, how I like to unburden my overflowing heart on paper this way. Sometimes I want to tear up the page, but why do that? I would just begin over again.
>
> At one moment I am so sure of myself that I believe that these dreams will become reality, and I forget the obstacles which block the road. But I do not think I can permit myself to

> believe that all the obstacles will disappear: this proves that I have a conscience. But let us come back to my hesitations. It is astonishing that it takes little or nothing to elate me. This evening I was reading the life of Fr. Lacordaire, and in his youth I found situations analogous to mine. He, too, loved solitude and did not confide his sentiments to anyone; he, too, loved the missions. Wouldn't it be the same for me? But, no matter what, let us always go ahead, with God's grace!
>
> But it is fine for me to shout: "Go ahead! With God's grace!" I still come back to my thoughts. At this time that is all that occupies my mind. It is already a year that I have been seriously seeking my way. I want to find my vocation, and a year has passed without my being able to solve the question. I foresee that a lot more time will go by before I will be sure. Maybe I will have decided by Easter. But why would I?
>
> Since last year I have certainly changed my ideas: I am a long way from the plans I made last year! What a difference there is between our former desires and those we have today! In the past, I wanted nothing but to enjoy the world: one could have said that I was going ahead enthusiastically to drown myself in the agitated waves of the world. But then I don't know what happened: probably grace put an end to this race and made me leave the world, not only high society but everything I hold dear to me in this world. And yet, in this change I notice that my spirit has not changed. I continue to have this ardour to advance toward danger, I want to go into combat. In the past I wanted to defend my country. I was a patriot. Today, I want to defend Jesus Christ. I want to conquer souls for him. I am a Christian!
>
> I want to leave the world. I want to consecrate myself to God. And yet, will I ever be certain? But here is the end of my anxieties: a letter just arrived for me from the Fathers of the Holy Spirit: "You can enter when you like."

He announced his decision to his father: leave the family's land to become a missionary. He apologized for having this audacity which some people might find very pretentious, and even more, for causing such chagrin to his family. However, "God speaks . . ." One must obey this call in spite of all the obstacles which reflection makes one see with respect to replying to such a high call. He counted on his father's consent to support his courage which was based solely on faith and hope in God. He had already taken the initiative to write to the Fathers of the Holy Spirit at Orly. The reply was positive:

> My dear Emmanuel,
>
> I am happy to be able to inform you of your admission to the novitiate of the Congregation. You can come as soon as you wish, September 28 at latest. Awaiting the pleasure of giving you a fraternal accolade, I ask the Lord to bless your trip.
>
> Your affectionate and devoted
> P. Grignard (August 30, 1898)

(At dawn messages were caught at sea . . .)
Such hope comes to life again in the bustle of the ports
That love of the sea and getting under sail
Is the meaning of the ship and of every setting out.

But each new departure knows a coming ashore
And the game begins again at the heart of the human heart
Which changes its destiny for another voyage.

From departure to departure the tomorrows wear thin
Illusion spreads from shore to shore
And foreseen regrets are at the end of the route.

You will know that life explains these mirages
When remorse soon bites into your hopes
And you gaze at the foam of the wake.

Thus will be exhausted our avidity to see
Everywhere, as in passing, the vague resemblance
Of our soul lost in this play of mirrors.

For looking at the sea is without meaning
The eye must listen to it with pure undertstanding
To approach being and bridge the distance.

Before all that is visible, before the firmament
A word was uttered where light was made:
This word of which you are made enlightens you intimately.

When his regard will see the One who spoke to him
And he will no longer have any words to say it
He will have become the voice who called him.

(. . . And the message at sea captured the ship).

C. D.

5

Leave your country and your father's house

So it was that at the station in Pontivy on the 20th of September Emmanuel took the 10:27 p.m. train for Paris. During his trip he wrote the following:

> Yes! Yes! The train is getting underway. It is my departure for Paris and the novitiate. It is my farewell to Brittany. Each puff of smoke that the locomotive gives off makes someone dear to me or some pleasant memory disappear from the horizon. It is my father, my aunt—why not say my mother—, it is my whole family which is disappearing. Everything is disappearing: after Séglien, it's Pontivy and Saint-Anne d'Auray. At Vannes there will be the Express train, and straight on to Paris! Goodbye, Vannes, with your peaceful streets and placid habitants! Goodbye, Nantes, who refuses to give way to night! It has replaced the sun by numerous electric lamp posts; work and agitation are without respite. Further off one can still see the high chimneys pouring forth their torrent of white smoke. Finally, here is the station: here it is brighter than in full daylight. But it is midnight and I haven't slept a wink. The train pulls out of the vast domed vaults of the station and goes along the banks of the Loire. But I give in. I stretch out and let my arms fall. I close my eyes and go to sleep. Suddenly I have changed pace: the tic-tac of the locomotive has given way to the sound of a horse's hoofs. I feel the jolts of the train. Then, all motion disappears. I am lying calmly in a soft bed at Loc-Ouviern. . . . No, I was dreaming. After this very pleasant nap of about one hour, I renounce falling again into the arms

of Morpheus. And yet, he was so kind: he took my consciousness away to spare me the sadness of passing the border of Brittany and seeing it disappear from the horizon. The countryside is very different now. Here is Blois, and Orléans with its vines. Here is the plain of Beauce which spreads out as far as one can see, with its bundles of wheat. Oh! My dear Brittany, where are your woods, your slopes covered with heather? Where are your gorse in flower and your green fields? It has disappeared with its picturesque sites and parceled-out fields. There, there is a shepherd who leads the little Breton calves and prods them along with his long stick; there is a peasant who holds on to his plough with a nervous hand; there is the crack of a whip. But what is there, further on, on the horizon? What a dark cloud! It is the outskirts of Paris, although not yet Paris itself. The red-roofed houses are crowded together, and the factories with their high chimneys belch forth unceasingly their thick clouds. Finally we cross the ditches and are in Paris. A new era is beginning for me now, because I am here in Paris. But Paris is Paris, whereas for me, I am a Breton from Brittany. But no matter . . . I jump into a closed carriage, and I arrive, invisible, at the Motherhouse, 30 rue Lhomond.

The next day I was permitted to pass the whole day in the capital of France; and I profited from it to show the metropolis the gleaming beauty of the silver buttons on my jacket.

So! Paris is Paris, I said to myself, and not Loc-Ouviern; and after comparing them I do not believe that Paris can outdo that little hamlet. But I must not have too much disdain for our capital. So I went out into the streets, to be able to speak about it fairly. Oh my! Right on Pont Street at Pontivy . . . Yes! I saw that it was trans . . . planted here, like a relic: it's the Latin Quarter. I shouldn't be surprised: latin is so old! And then, I came to a wide street. Ah! Here, it's death. I pass between two carriages coming toward me from opposite directions at a gallop. I am stopped by a third one in the middle of the street, and by a fourth am obliged to jump aside. Then I am splashed by an automobile. Finally I get back on the sidewalk. There, at least, I will be at ease. But jostled about by a hundred people, I am pushed against sidewalk stands and then pushed back in the other direction a thousand times against piles of the stevedores' crates. Ah! Paris! It certainly is amusing!

> I do not think that the streets in Loc-Ouviern are as cluttered up as that. So I was right to say that Paris does not surpass Loc-Ouviern. Fortunately, however, Paris is more than that. There are Notre-Dame, the Pantheon, and so many beautiful monuments. Notre-Dame with its magnificent façade all in sculpture, like lace; it is so beautiful that our kings have their niches there along with the saints. I saw the *Sainte Chapelle*, as svelte as a young Breton girl in her holiday dress; it is all lace and embroidery. Through the fog I got a glimpse of Madame Eiffel Tower, but I have not yet condescended to empty my cart of homage at her feet. I went up to Montmartre: the church of the Sacred Heart. It is so beautiful, so touching!
>
> But Paris and I are two different things, because I come from Brittany, my fatherland, the most beautiful country after heaven. But let's not talk about that anymore.
>
> I have said adieu to it. Adieu, Breiz-Isel. Adieu.

Inserting this long quotation here has been useful inasmuch as it enables us to weigh what Emmanuel's uprooting and saying goodbye to his dear Brittany meant to him. It also helps us to discover this young boy's extreme sensitivity, which long years of monastic life and being abbot would never really succeed in hiding. Still—and this is another aspect of his personality that would not fade away either—since he had said Adieu, he would accept with honesty and openness the demands of his detachment.

6

Here finally lies the old man

And in fact, on September 29, 1898, there was great serenity.

> Today, at 11 a.m., I was clothed with a cassock. I cannot express how much my heart was filled with joy. I am happy to wear the livery of Jesus Christ. But I must be worthy to wear it, at least insofar as I am able. With my whole being I must apply myself to getting rid of my imperfections, so that I may be worthy to celebrate the Holy Sacrifice of the Mass and proclaim Jesus' words to pagans. During my novitiate the means I should employ is conformity to the rules: accomplish the whole rule, all perfection is there. But it is not enough to accomplish the rule in just any way. I should not confine myself to its material side. I should not be simply a slave. I am here because God led me on, but by my own will. I came here with the intention of trying to become perfect, to make reparation for my faults and to gain heaven. So let's have some good will. Furthermore, I didn't invent any illusions: I am finding what I wanted and I am delighted with it. I want to give myself to God completely: body and soul, my strength and freedom, health and spirit, everything, everything. I no longer have any belongings, my parents are far away from me. I am lost to them. I have only to follow Jesus. I surrender to him and I no longer want anything but to do his will.

During the first months of his novitiate he was filled with joy and wonder:

> So many instructions, so many consolations! Every day brings something new and makes me progress in my knowledge of

> God's gifts. And each day I try to leave behind me a part of the old man, so that I can replace it by something better, patterned on my model Jesus Christ. That way, some day I may be able to say: "Ego sum alter Christus." What a year, then, this 1898 is! And without any boasting I can regard it as being worth something before God's eyes. And what will 1899 bring? I am on the right way, but what will happen? Joys, sorrows, anguish, peace, departure, dismissal, sickness, death? Mystery! Mystery!!! May your will be done in all things, my God!

The young novice added to this first summary a drawing of a tombstone bearing the inscription: "Here lies the old man 1898," whereas another drawing represents a theatre curtain bearing the date 1899 and has the following heading: "The 21st Act of my life. What will it bring? The curtain has not yet gone up. Mystery! God presides. Death listens and awaits the appointed time." Here, anyone who later knew Dom Anselme is already smiling with delight at the resolute and marvelous funny side of him as a person. This somewhat clownish aspect of his character would later on spare him from the grip of bitterness toward an ecclesiastical and monastic hierarchy which was too pompously pontifical to suit him, and sometimes narrow and even unjust.

The first three months of his novitiate therefore offered Emmanuel hours of peace and purity, so pleasant that in order to enjoy them fully he felt obliged to think back over the storm which had preceded such calmness. From a strictly psychological point of view one could think it was masochistic. From a spiritual point of view, we find ourselves rather before the remembrance of this passover by which God made him go beyond darkness to his admirable light. Emmanuel's lucidity is astonishing. The following lines were written on the evening of December 31, 1898.

> 1898 is over, with its interminable 365 days, each one counting its full 24 hours. Tic tac, went my watch; tic tac, the year is going by; tic, tac, the year has gone by. Here we are on December 31. Now, when I want to examine these interminable 365 days, I have a very hard time distinguishing the different parts,

like when someone awakes from a dream. No matter: considered as a whole, my memories of it are good, and with no mistake I can look at it as a year that has value before God's eyes. Alas! It is the first, it is the only one which can have any worth for me in eternity, the only one of the 20 years that I have passed on earth. And yet, I have not done anything by myself, I have just corresponded to graces from heaven: conversion, vocation, perseverance, all that in one single year! Oh! How many changes have come about in me, what a brusque about-face in my life! It is only now that I can see it, it is now that the perspective permits me to judge properly the gratuity of God's gifts.

In what state was I? In what state am I now? Born into a Christian family, I showed my gratitude to my Creator by offending him in the worst way: by impurity. Ever since I was young there was passion, and it kept growing as I advanced in life. Passion blinded me and hardened my heart. Still, when classes started in October, 1896, after a retreat I had a glimmer of hope. I was converted, but only for three months. My relapse was serious and at the same time I sank into a more miserable state than before my change. In 1897 I was at the paroxysm of my passion. It was no longer the attraction of mild passion but the torture of an insatiable gratification. I was in love, and I ingeniously contrived bad dreams, to the point of making that a continual habit. I was impure in my whole being.

It was on this foundation that I had to build my vocation. Actually it preoccupied me, and mixed in with bad thoughts it found its orientation. So it was a matter of finding a state of life which could accord with my passions and even be favorable to them. But God permits—I realize this now—those who go astray not to lose completely the sentiments which He imprinted in their original nature as signs of their vocation. The ideas of dedication and sacrifice were to me something general and an ideal to accomplish. I found an expression of them in the soldier who devotes himself to the service of his country, and who sacrifices his life to defend his compatriots. I found it especially in someone who leaves his family and country and goes far away to make France known and loved. What a wonderful career! Briefly, I resolved to become a soldier. The dream was easy, but how I could carry it out caused me doubts and anxiety, and my plans fell apart only to start all over again more forcefully. This alternation of joys and sad daydreams gave vent to my passions and filled me with a distaste for the priestly life that went as far as scorn. The long vacation made it worse and if I had been able to do so I would have abandoned the Minor Seminary. So I returned with heavy sadness. It was not my place, but it was impossible for me to find a remedy at that time. I spent the retreat at the beginning of the school year in a state of boredom and distaste for spiritual practices. Had I not gone as low as possible? But it is when everything seems lost that God intervenes and by his grace gives the final blow.

So it was that on Sunday, November 7, 1897, about 7 o'clock in the evening, according to the custom there was a sermon at the Minor Seminary of Saint-Anne. Mister Breléon, my director, preached that evening. He took the following text as his subject: "*Transiit benefaciendo*," and by happy circumstance applied it to a young seminarian seeking his vocation. With the seminarian, he described the various careers which could attract him, and each time he always finished with this lesson: "Live in a way that one can say of you: *Transiit benefaciendo* . . . He passed by doing good." At first I listened to this list more or less attentively, more for its literary beauty than for the salutary instruction that it was. Then, as the priest's words became more forceful, his ardor woke me up and captivated my spirit, and I started to think vaguely about my condition while defying the preacher to touch me, so to speak. His list continued: "Ah, as for me, I will be a soldier," one young man will say. "I want glory for my country. That's a noble cause! It is dangerous in our times, but one can do good that way. Go, pass by doing good." Another one will say: "As for me, I want to be a missionary to save my soul, and the souls of pagans. I want to pass by doing good."

Suddenly I felt very upset. With my dreams, I had no place in these groups. So I was a useless being. Immediately, and at the same time, without my being able to realize it, I made the twofold resolution to work at my conversion and to become a missionary. I was beside myself. I became enthusiastic, and even outwardly overexcited. It was like a light which blinded me and yet clearly showed me the road that I should follow, and consequently what I should leave behind. Even today I do not know how that happened: it was God's grace which overwhelmed me. And from where did this new sign of God's infinite goodness come to me? On account of me? Oh, no! I had so often refused his graces. Was it because of my aunt, who was a religious and prayed for me? Was it because of one of my friends who asked God to make me a priest? All that is a mystery. I hope that my gratitude to God will reach out to everyone who has been good to me. I was converted at last, and sincerely. It was not without future combat, however, because a man does not change completely in the twinkling of an eye.

So it happened that three months later, without any transition, I again found myself plunged into doubt and anxiety: work became more laborious, and time, in itself, was unable to deliver me from these things. It was in this atmosphere that my vocation came to me. I worked first by reasoning. Rejecting the fantasies of my dreams that I had recently woven on purpose and whose falseness I was aware of, I applied myself to considering only what was most repulsive in the apostolic life: being far away from my homeland, separation from my family, the physical sufferings in the missions, and especially the moral sufferings. I was capable of enduring all these things, and in my opinion I even should endure them to make reparation for my sins and save my soul. To this reasoning I added prayer. I prayed and fervently asked God "to accept me in his troops." I pleaded impetuously with Him as well as with the Blessed Virgin, but I could not resign myself to saying from the bottom of my heart, even though I said it with my lips: "May your will be done in all things." I wanted to be a missionary, and I even cried out: "I have found my way!"

But could the devil let go of me without some mischief-making? Old Nick is not so conciliating. This sly one attacked me underhandedly. Really, I said to myself, after such a life as mine can I be a priest? Would you dare to touch the Body of Jesus with your sinful hands? At one moment I was absolutely sure of succeeding; at the next moment I fell into the deepest despair. Always the same alternative, always the desire to reach the end of the year. The devil thought he could lead me astray that way.

Finally, the year drew to a close and, without asking anyone's advice and without telling anyone, I immediately applied for admission to the Congregation of the White Fathers. Then came

July 26. My aunt, whom I saw that day, was not thrilled at all about my decision: she wanted me to enter the Congregation of the Holy Spirit and Holy Heart of Mary. That same day my director also said he was favorable to that. As for me, since I was indifferent about both congregations, urged by grace I willingly consented to their desire. So it happened that on August 15, 1898, I asked to enter the novitiate of the Fathers of the Holy Spirit. But what anxiety I still had while waiting for an answer. Finally, it arrived. Oh, what joy I felt at that moment: I was full of happiness, and cried out: "Here is the answer to all my previous anxiety. The end of the year arrived and here is what happened. Glory be to God!"

7

A calm and rapid Spiritan novitiate

After this long and courageous account which Emmanuel wrote during the evening of December 31, 1898, his personal notes became more infrequent and more brief. This sobriety reflects the atmosphere of his novitiate, during which he wrote, "life flows along rapid and calm." He waited until Ash Wednesday, February 15, 1899, before taking up his pen again and relishing in a certain way the serenity which he felt at last:

> I find that time goes by so quickly. At college, it was nothing but eternity upon eternity; and yet there was no lack of things to do. But here I find that time escapes me too quickly and one has the impression that we have nothing to do. In college I was not in my place: you hope, you desire what you dream of, and boredom takes over in that transitory state. Here I am beginning a way of existing which will last all my life. The practices of the novitiate are the Rule. And no matter what our exterior action may be, these practices remain the foundation. That way, a person is in his place and everything goes along well. Little by little one forgets one's country, family and friends, at least to the extent that this is permitted and reasonable. One is no longer preoccupied with mulling these things over. Saying goodbye is finished, and one gives himself completely to God and to the Congregation, his spiritual family, without looking back. What a beautiful time! It is astonishing how this great work of the novitiate takes place: one's spiritual progress. That is because from now on I can look upon myself as someone who is called. I am happy to have found the religious life in

> this Congregation without having searched for it. I came here almost blindly and now that I am here I see that it was the only place that was right for me.

The letters Emmanuel wrote to his family had exactly the same tone: "Life goes on here, always more rapid, calm and consoling." Spiritual work, with prayer, took up all his time. His family was not to send him anything. The virtue of poverty had taken its place among his religious obligations. Furthermore, they should not worry about him; he had everything he needed. "I have found what I was looking for," he liked to repeat. He had only one desire, for which he asked prayers from his family: to become a good religious and good missionary.

He made his first vows in October, 1899, after preparing himself by a retreat. Unfortunately, his retreat notes are nothing but very precise summaries of the retreat master's instructions. They leave no trace of introspection or personal examination of conscience, as though he had decided to let himself be guided by the objective means of the religious Rule, without including what he was experiencing in his soul. In this respect, his resolution at the end of the retreat is significant:

> I am making the resolution to observe our Rule in a spirit of faith: to do each thing at its appointed time, do each thing in union with God. Naturalism, in fact, killed me; faith should save me. And I believe that in order to snuff out naturalism, exact observance of the Rule is, in itself, an important means. That way I will extinguish ardor of the flesh, while forming my will and character. Because strict observance of the Rule will influence my way of reasoning, I will employ reason with regard to the Rule, and as I reason I will put the spirit of faith into it. Still, since the flesh remains and flesh is not spirit, one must subdue it so that the spirit may be predominant. In order to maintain my regular observance of the Rule, I therefore also make this resolution: to mortify myself by frequently making the Way of the Cross—every day if possible—and by depriving myself in various ways. Everything should be foreseen during my particular examination of conscience, and accomplished

> without fail, once the circumstance is determined. May God bless my resolutions and give me the grace to accomplish them, by the intercession of Mary Most Holy, towards whom I owe a particular devotion.

Knowing that several years later he was going to enter La Trappe, where at that time strict observance of the *Usages and Customs* was sacred, we can guess that there, too, at Scourmont, at the beginning he would put his complete confidence in the healing power of the rules. However, because he had already been subject to rules for several years before becoming a Trappist novice, he would discover sooner than other novices the snares of such a yoke, and would have the spiritual freedom to look at them as being relative; or more exactly, would make them serve charity. Because, as he wrote during his novitiate: "The perfection glimpsed at the first moment no longer suffices; one must go higher. It is a question of acquiring the spirit of the Congregation, a spirit which we find in the life of the founder: charity."

> One must love his brothers, put up with their faults, live with them in very great familiarity. No more nationality, no more compatriots, no more co-disciples, no more special affinities because of natural equality or character. From now on there is one single family: *Cor unum et anima una*. By the action of grace one no longer seeks oneself. One lives in a spiritual family, and finds himself happy. One forgets oneself little by little so as to see only brothers.

If up until now the reader may have felt a sort of uneasiness about Emmanuel's insistence on observing the Regulations, we can be reassured when we read in his notes that observances have but one goal: to free us from self-love and self-will so that we may be able to love others. Is this not the way proposed by Saint Benedict, which Brother Anselme would later discover and value?

Leaving oneself is an even more dangerous adventure than leaving one's country. Emmanuel, whom spiritual combat had caused to mature, acknowledged this:

> God has made a light shine. Even if He disappears from time to time, the road remains passable. I do not stop and I do not cry. I have to struggle all the time, but the struggle is frank and joyful. And when my spirits are low I still have the joy of suffering in communion with Jesus Christ. I see now that leaving one's parents, cherished friends and country is nothing: leaving oneself is much more difficult. But let's go ahead courageously for the love of God and of souls. What a beautiful life!

After such a pleasant and short novitiate, Emmanuel was admitted to pronounce his first vows. Dom Anselme preserved his profession formula preciously:

> Today, October 10, 1899, on the feast of Saint Francis of Borgia, in the chapel of the religious house of the Sacred Heart, at Grignon Orlof, in presence of the Community, I, the undersigned, have made my religious profession, according to the following formula:
>
>> In the name of the Father and of the Son and of the Holy Spirit. Amen.
>
> Most holy and very adorable Trinity, penetrated with the most ardent gratitude for the precious favor you have deigned to accord me in calling me to the religious and apostolic life, I come with happiness to consecrate myself to your divine Majesty.
>
> With the desire, O my God, to belong to you forever, before this holy altar I present to you the entire gift of myself, in this pious Congregation which accepts to receive me among its members; and by love for you I abandon to it my freedom, my health and my life, willing to immolate myself without any reservations to the sacred interests of your glory.
>
> With this purpose I commit myself above all to work unceasingly toward my own perfection, and at the same time to devote myself with zeal to the salvation and sanctification of my neighbor, especially the most forsaken souls.
>
> I commit myself, finally, to persevere throughout my whole life in the Congregation as a faithful and devoted member, in spite of deceitful solicitations of my nature, the world and the

devil. I declare, particularly, that I will not consider the afflictions and trials which may befall me to be legitimate motives for abandoning my vocation; rather, with the grace of God I will strive to bear them with patience and resignation, like our Divine Master did, in view of my own sanctification and the salvation of my neighbor.

O Holy Spirit, to whom I have the happiness of being henceforth consecrated, pour into my soul an abundance of your graces, gifts of wisdom and understanding, of counsel and strength, of knowledge, piety and fear of God; and penetrate my heart with the courage and zeal with which you filled the Apostles, so that I may constantly follow their footsteps.

And you, O Divine Mary, Mother of mercy and goodness, support my weakness, and obtain for me the grace always to accomplish my holy commitments with generosity, so that after a life of fervour and holiness I may join, in heaven and for eternity, the children of your immaculate Heart, in the glory of the Father, the Son and the Holy Spirit. Amen.

After pronouncing these obligations toward the Congregation, I made my first vows of religion, according to the following formula:

> In the name of the Father and of the Son and of the Holy Spirit. Amen.

In the presence of Our lord Jesus Christ, of the Most Blessed Virgin, of the Holy Patrons of the Congregation, and of all the saints in heaven, I, Emmanuel Jean Marie LE BAIL, make, for three years, the vow of Poverty, of Chastity and Obedience, in the Congregation of the Holy Spirit and the Holy Heart of Mary, and in conformity with its Rules and Constitutions.

In testimony whereof, this same day I have signed two copies of the present Act.

Given at Grignon-Orlof, the 10th day of the month of October, eighteen hundred ninety-nine.

Emmanuel Jean Marie Le Bail
(Seal of the Community, by the Superior, P. Lorber)

8

A soldier of Christ in an army on earth

An interruption occurred in this life that was so calm. In November Emmanuel was called up for military service. This prospect of a year's delay in his anxious waiting to become a priest and leave for Africa was not very good news to him, even though—as he stated—he did not fear it "in any way." Should we not submit to civil laws, which are an expression of God's will? So he put aside his cassock as a young professed religious to "put on red breeches." 1900: the beginning of a century. Our second-class soldier accomplished his military service at Lorient. Not everything was rosy for him in this new life, so different from his ideal. In a letter dating from the beginning of March, he wrote to his father after being sick and spending some time in the infirmary:

> God does well what he does . . . and the Major, too. I have returned to service, and things are going all right, except that my feet hurt when I have to march 20 kilometers with a pack on my back. It was hard for me to get back in the ranks. I was clumsy, all my limbs were like they were crippled and they yelled at me as if I were a donkey. But, bah! Everything comes to an end. God lives on, all the same. Maturin is going on leave to Séglien. I do not get favors from the Captain like he does, so I will not go with him. I get my name in the Captain's papers only when it has to do with punishments. But everything will end, and after that there will be happiness.

There was a new letter in July, several months later: all the enlisted men had a 25-day leave to go home, but our Emmanuel who was absent from the Company and was not told about it until it was too late could not take advantage of this good luck, no doubt because a leave required an application ahead of time. He concluded with a bit of melancholy:

> In the army a man does not do simply what he wants. . . . I stayed at my assigned post by duty, a post for a lazy fellow if there ever was one. I sleep and walk around. That has been my only occupation this month. . . .

When his year of service was over, he received a certificate of excellence from the chaplain to give to his superiors: "I have not the slightest complaint to mention about him, everything just the opposite."

In his personal notes Emmanuel made a spiritual evaluation of this year:

> Most of the year 1900 has been spent on the army base. A sad life. I do not want to remember anything about it. If I have had the occasion to offer some sufferings to God for the expiation of my sins and the salvation of souls, I thank Him. I have been weak. I found out that I am miserable, and I ask God's forgiveness. Finally the Sacred Heart sent me back safe and sound to my Congregation. So I want to thank him and forget the past so that I may be able to set out again on my way, the one I should follow. I will undertake it again—just as I will thank God for preparing me for the work he wants to give me—by living for him alone and sanctifying myself in order to sanctify others. That's what my work will be. While thinking about this goal in a general manner, I have no desire to try to figure out the future. I have no desires for it except what God wants it to be. Let's be contented with the present, and leave the rest to God! I thought I would finish in four years, and become a priest in three years. They want me to take two years of philosophy. I want that, too, my God. The voice of my Superiors directs me to prepare a bachelor's degree. I will do it, my God. I will wait until I will be almost twenty-six years old before becoming a priest. I submit in everything to the will of God. Let's look only at the present for now and see how to sanctify it, and live it in

union with God. Holiness consists in union with God by the accomplishment of his will. So I have only to observe the Rule for God, and to observe it for Him alone; and I will not be wasting my time.

9

Missionary, seminarian, savior of souls

From 1901 until 1903, Emmanuel Le Bail kept few notes about how things were developing for him. Besides, he had perhaps stopped this type of introspection in order to study more objectively the demands of the priesthood, on which he was resolutely decided. The year 1901 was a year of philosophy at the house for Scholastics in Chevilly, which he finished by an examination in philosophy at the Sorbonne. The years 1902 and 1903 were consecrated to theology. They ended in July, with his receiving the four minor orders.

If we want to have some idea of his daily life during these years, here is a precise description of it:

> 5 a.m.: Rise promptly, and preparation for prayer.—5:15: Prayer. Consideration of the subject. Implore Jesus and Mary frequently. Thrust of the soul toward God. Simple resolution, with an act to accomplish during the day—6 a.m.: My room. Prepare to attend Mass and receive Holy Communion—6h:15: Mass. Offering. Intention. Union with the priest in reciting the liturgical prayers. When I do not receive Communion, during and after Communion, recite the Litany of the Sacred Heart and consecration to the Sacred Heart. Thank God for the grace of attending Mass. Ask his forgiveness insofar as I may have assisted poorly at Mass and abused grace. When I receive Communion, thanksgiving, adoration, gratitude. Pardon with the help of Mary and my patron saints. Give myself to Jesus. Magnificat. Pray for the Church, for the Congregation, for my family, for the souls in Purgatory—7h: Work on philosophy. In

all my work I ought to put aside my rather natural and quite strong attraction to study. I should work because God wants me to. I will show God that I will work for Him, by putting aside study for prayer when it is time, with the same ease that I put aside prayer for study—7:30: Breakfast. During the meal, do not give my attention to anything but the reading, while rendering little services to my neighbors.—7:45: Recreation. Practise charity.—8 a.m.: Visit to the chapel. Make the offering of my work to God. Pray for the light of the Holy Spirit.—8:30: Class. A lot of attention: God wants it.—9:30: Short visit to the Blessed Sacrament, to thank Him and ask Him to help me understand one or another thing said in class. Work on philosophy, sciences or history.—11 a.m.–11:45: Class. Examination of conscience. Ask Jesus to help me recognize my faults, to forgive me for them and to give me the means to correct them. Resolution. Give myself a penance for whatever was not quite correct—12 noon: Rosary on the way to the refectory. Dinner. *Miserere*, coming back.—12:30 p.m.: recreation.—1 p.m.: Manual work. Whatever I am asked to do, do it for God. Union with Jesus working during his hidden life—1:45 p.m.: Rosary. Intention. Attention. Meditation.—2 o'clock: work on philosophy.—3:30: class—4:30: recreation—4:45: meeting. Attention as keen and serious as in class—5 p.m.: A rather long visit to the Blessed Sacrament. Spiritual reading, Scripture—6:30: conference—7 p.m.: visit to the Blessed Sacrament. Adoration. Veneration of Jesus-Eucharist, by Mary, the guardian of Jesus-Host, priest par excellence. Ask Mary to help me love the Holy Eucharist, so that I may become a good priest, guardian and companion of Jesus in the tabernacle. The profit I can gain from the conference—7:15: supper and recreation—8:30: prayer—8:45: preparation of the next day's prayer. Prayer at my bedside.—9 p.m.: Go to bed. Preparation for death.

In the moments of transition from one occupation to another, in stray moments, never let my imagination wander. I must ask God's pardon if my preceding action has been poorly done and thank Him if it has been well done. Offer (Him) what I have to do next and plan my use of time. Think about my studies, too; go back over what has been seen and prepare what is to be studied next. Make a spiritual communion often.

My soul, love God and go on your way.

Our contemporary sensibility is stupefied by this rhythm of daily life, where not one minute is left to chance or imagination. It was that way in all the religious Congregations at that time, and no doubt Brother Anselme found these same minute details during his first years at La Trappe. We notice first of all the type of spirituality characteristic of the beginning of the century: Eucharistic devotion to Jesus-Host in the tabernacle, the priest being his guardian and companion; devotion to Mary by frequent recitation of the rosary; constant preoccupation about receiving pardon for one's sins; the thought of death.

Another characteristic of this spirituality consisted in living constantly "in presence of God," not only during moments of prayer, of course, or in "stray moments of transition," but even during intellectual activity. This desire to live continually in presence of God, which took on an almost obsessive character exteriorly, no doubt conceals great finesse of heart: that is, never really leaving the God one loves, asking his pardon for the slightest infidelities, and thanking him for the thousands of graces he gives.

Lastly, we can imagine what astonishing will power such a style required, and what great concentration of all of a person's energy. In this domain, we perhaps feel permitted to have some suspicion about the amount of voluntarism which inevitably entered into the formation of these young religious; it is as though they were forbidden to bother about themselves too much so as to be able to conform exclusively to the ideal proposed to them.

We have some reason to think so, when in the young Le Bail's notes dating from that period we read certain resolutions repeated over and over again in large letters: "I must become a priest, a good priest, one who saves souls, a victim: I must!"

These strongly-phrased resolutions, like others found elsewhere, conclude the notes he wrote during a retreat on the priesthood. When we look through them we discover things we already know about the theology of the priesthood at the end of the nineteenth century and the beginning of the twentieth: a certain type of image of the priest. This image was certainly not heterodox, but the theology of the Second Vatican Council fortunately restored the priest to his place at the heart of the People of God, also priestly and mediative, in the service of the One High Priest Jesus Christ. Here, the perspective is individual, circumscribed and sacrificial.

> First, we were shown the priest in the dignity of his mission, established by God to serve men in whatever concerns Divine Cult, to offer sacrifices of propitiation and thanksgiving for himself and for others, responsible for leading the souls who are entrusted to him to God. I saw the beauty of his vocation: to lead souls to God, and creatures to the infinitely perfect Being. I saw the power he has at his disposal to accomplish his mission. He commands heaven and hell, on this earth, and God obeys him. From a little bread and several drops of wine he makes a God, Jesus, really present in the Holy Species after Consecration. This thought makes me tremble. I, too, will be a priest. I will be clothed with this dignity, and I will consecrate. I, vile sinner that I am, I will consecrate. It is a state in which I cannot imagine myself. These hands, so often soiled, will hold the Body of Jesus. I think about this, I try to convince myself, and instinctively I draw back my hands, I hide them, they burn me, I might say. They will not be able to support this weight. And the conclusion that I draw from this is that I imagine it will never happen to me. This impure mouth become an instrument of consecration! In the past it pronounced only words of death, and soon it will pronounce words of Life; it will bestow corporal existence upon Being par excellence, it will make Jesus Christ. Is it possible for me? But this problem has already tormented me. Today, since God's grace has instructed me, let us resign ourselves and pray. If it pleases God to call me to this mystery, I will go ahead; and if he asks me only for my good will, I will still be satisfied. For the time being I must act in presence of reality and prepare myself for the priesthood.
>
> I come back to my studies. In this state of dignity, the priest should not see anything but God and souls. God has elevated him, but it is not a grace for him alone. It is not enough for him to be in admiration and self-annihilation before the divine action. If God has raised him up, it is so that he may look after his interests and those of souls. Everything that a priest does outside of this goal is disorder and monstrosity. That is the real-

> ity. That is God! (N.B. That is the theme of this retreat: the priest, God-Man). Is not the priest, in fact, a God? He remains none the less a man. Happy would he be if he would be a man like Jesus Christ was: a suffering man, a man struggling and triumphing. Alas, the priest can be a man who is a sinner. Even though he receives the priestly character, even though he becomes another Christ, a God, he nevertheless keeps his bad nature. He still has his human character, his flesh prone to concupiscence, his weakness, his passions. The devil does not attack him any less than before; he doubles his trickery and hate in the measure that God gives his graces. He attacks him as a priest, he attacks him as a simple man. Souls are no longer attractive to him, but rather, by the action of the devil they appear more vile, more repulsive. God himself seems to abandon him, and tests him in order to increase his merits. But on the other hand the priest receives a very great abundance of graces, and when he falls he sins more seriously. No one else sins with greater malice. It is a Christ who sins. He, the way, the truth and the life, gives himself as such, and in sin he goes astray, he errs and kills himself. And while he announces to souls that he is the way, the truth and the life, he leads them astray and into error, and kills them. He has the responsibility to do good by what he is; his mission is to destroy sin and evil, by the sacraments of Baptism and Penance, and yet he himself does evil! A fallen priest is a monster.

It seems clear that the preceding discourse did not come from Emmanuel, but from the priest who preached the retreat, faithfully transcribed. The lines which follow seem to be more personal and do seem to come from Emmanuel, who was trying to get away from this particularly terrifying picture by referring to the theological virtues of Faith, Hope and especially Love, which can save the priest from the greatest dangers.

> The priest has a supernatural mission, and acts only for God. This thought is his guide and light. To this spirit of Faith he adds Hope, which supports him in his renouncement. And above all, he will love souls, because Faith and Hope need to be founded on Love. Voluntary and complete sacrifice requires love.

O Holy Spirit, hasten to make me know this Love, to make it understood, to put it into practice. It is the love of Jesus Christ for us. O Saint John, apostle of Charity, the beloved disciple, be my guide.

God is calling me to the priestly life: He is giving me a great grace. He is calling me to the religious, priestly life, and this is a still greater gift. God wants me to be a religious so that I may sacrifice myself more completely for his glory. The vows will make me a victim immolated for the salvation of souls. But still, it is I who must immolate myself, it is for me to save souls.

Crucified Jesus, my model, my love, I place my resolution at your feet, and I ask you for the strength to accomplish it. O crucified Jesus, I must be a good priest. And to become one I must not neglect anything in my preparation: accomplishing the Rule, I will be a victim; learning everything for you and living for you, in you, with you, in all things I will be a good priest, a crucified savior, a saver of souls. I must!

10

A sudden shadow on tranquil happiness

In October, 1903, Emmanuel finished his first three years of studies and normally should have made his vows for five years. But he was preoccupied about his future and one can detect some hesitation at this time. In July he had received the four minor Orders from Msgr. Leroy, Superior General of the Congregation. Now he was on the point of acceding to the diaconate, and he was hesitating. He asked if he could make a retreat, to think about it. What happened exactly we do not know. But following the advice of his director he put off going ahead to Holy Orders. This was a disappointment for his family—he was very conscious of that—but as he saw it, it was the will of God at that moment. He should therefore submit to it.

There was something else: since he was not yet a sub-deacon he found himself caught up by the military laws and obliged to finish the two years of service which remained for him to complete. He asked, therefore, to go back to his family in the hope of taking advantage of certain influences which would free him from these burdensome obligations. It would seem that these influences produced positive results. So there he was back at Séglien, but with the project of later joining one of the works of the Congregation of the Holy Spirit in order to test his vocation for two or three years. But things went fast and on January 26, 1904, he was dismissed from the Congregation by a decision of the Superior General because of his prolonged hesitations, and for this reason alone. For in a letter sent to Dom Norbert of Scourmont, the Superior of the Spiritans said he was "jealous" when he learned that such a "good element" had been taken away from them by the Trappists.

He spent several months with his family, a period that we could call a retreat in the midst of his deeply Christian family who supported him with their prayer and spiritual understanding. In May, 1904, he made a long retreat at the Cistercian Abbey of Timadeuc, about 20 kilometers from Kervégan, Neuillac.

Unfortunately none of his personal notes from this period are extant; they would have let us know the reason for Emmanuel's rapid decision to become a Trappist monk, and why he preferred Notre-Dame de Saint-Joseph Abbey, Scourmont, in far-off Belgium, to the Abbey of Timadeuc. Was it perhaps in order to follow literally the Gospel advice to leave everything, homeland and family? In any case, he made no reference to this. He knocked on the door of Scourmont on May 21, in the year 1904.

11

La Trappe: A first-class burial

He left without saying goodbye to his family, but eight days later wrote to his father:

> I have once again found the same joy and cheerfulness I knew in the old days. In the world people talk a lot about La Trappe, but they know very little about it. Beneath the Cistercian's habit the world sees nothing but a man who weeps all the time and a body that suffers. Materially speaking, of course, the Cistercian does not pass his life in pleasant enjoyment. Actually, it is a life that is quite hard, especially in the long run, when one knows that for twenty years, without any change in the timetable and without any hope of something unexpected, one will be subject to exactly the same set of rules. And yet, with God's grace one can embrace this life joyfully and find in it a kind of happiness which could not be attained in a life where capriciousness is the rule.

While no doubt wanting to reassure his father, Emmanuel—henceforth Brother Anselme—seems to have known what he was getting into and not to have joined the Trappists on the spur of the moment. He wrote to a friend: "It's a first-class burial." To his family he wrote more soberly:

> Here, during this last week, I have had eight different jobs. A person submits to such occupations only by necessity or by God's grace. My education and instruction pushed me toward studying; I am making in part a sacrifice, and in part humiliation of my nature by manual work, so as to expiate for myself

> and others. But I expect a lot of my present state. I didn't merit this grace from God. Implore him earnestly for my perseverance, and be persuaded that you are praying for my happiness, even here below. Because life at La Trappe, lived for God, procures joy and even pleasure.

He described his land of exile as flat, wooded country. French was spoken there, and furthermore a good number of the religious were French. He added, not without a bit of irony and bitterness: "One is so assured of the future in this gentle country of France!" All the same he missed his beloved homeland, but in the cloister he felt content and happy. There is another significant avowal in a letter to his aunt: "I came here like someone condemned to death; the truth is that I was both the executioner and the victim!" But this lovable aunt should remain in peace, because he knew that she was sad about this change: "Except for the Divine Office and the poetry of fresh summer mornings, it is true that my nature finds no attraction to the rhythm of this life. Seven hours of sleep can of course be enough, but I would prefer to go to bed at two o'clock in the morning and get up at eight o'clock. In the beginning I could not get to sleep before midnight. With the help of fatigue however, I have quickly gotten into the habit of sleeping any time of the day or night." Always reassuring his aunt about his health, at the end of December he wrote to her: "I feel marvellous. Although you might think the opposite, this rhythm of life is very fortifying; everything is in the right proportion. We get exercise and everything is foreseen by the rules. So I am much more robust than I was during my last stay at Séglien."

12

To love one's family is a virtue

Who was Brother Anselme's Novice Master at this time? Whoever he was, he must have been a Trappist monk with a very open mind and a big heart, permitting as he did his novice Anselme to maintain such frequent contact with his family. It was surely his Novice Master who permitted him to get away from the "fierce intransigence of the Desert Fathers." Brother Anselme wrote to his family: "Today there is no longer the same mentality, and I have been rightly told that to show natural affection to one's relatives is a virtue. This is also the spirit that I want to have. And if you come so far as to my solitude, you will be joyfully and cordially welcomed." He of course refrained from all contact during Advent, but his letter to his father at Christmas overflowed with affection:

> We like to think of those we love as being the same as we are, and to wish for them what we are and what we have, when these things are good. I feel good in my monastery, so I wish you a life a bit like mine, in your own house. As I wrote to auntie, the life you both lead is a little bit like the life of a monk: you have a life of prayer, reading and manual work. Your house is set rather apart from others; the church is nearby: that makes a monastery. We could call it Notre-Dame of Saint-Joseph of Séglien. We are alike and our lot is truly a happy one!

Besides his keeping in touch by correspondence, there were also his family's visits to the abbey. There was the visit of his aunt, who travelled 800 kilometers to see her nephew in the parlor of the abbey. They had spiritual conversations which lasted for hours, and afterwards continued to develop their subjects of discussion more deeply by correspondence. There was also the visit of his father after four years of separation. Five years would go by before they would see one another again, for the last time, at Dom Anselme's abbatial blessing.

For the moment, let us put aside the chronological sequence of Brother Anselme's life and continue to look through the letters he wrote to his family. At the time of his ordination to the priesthood in August, 1909, Fr. Anselme showed that he had distanced himself from his family, as was normal for someone in the monastic life. No one in his family was present at his ordination, following the desire that he himself had discreetly expressed:

> I will not insist on your coming. If you come I will be happy to see that you are happy. If you do not come, I will still be happy, but especially for myself. Because in these circumstances a person likes to be alone and not to be taken up by exterior things, so as to be completely absorbed with the grace that one is receiving. So choose. Whatever you choose, I will in any case be happy about it.

Actually, his family did not come to Scourmont. But by a letter dated September 5 he sent his blessing as a new priest to all his relatives. In this letter nothing gives us a glimpse of his impressions and feelings. "The best thing to do is to remain quiet and thank God in silent adoration. Be united to me in the future by frequent eucharistic communion."

A year later, on the anniversary of his ordination to the priesthood, he wrote to his father:

> Auntie wrote me that you live more and more like a monk. You do that no doubt to rival me: I am very happy about it. Soon you will be going to Timadeuc: once a year, to make a spiritual retreat. That is a good idea and would be a good custom. You would be well received there, and could taste for a while the charm of life at La Trappe.

In the meantime his aunt fell seriously ill, this aunt who had brought him up and whom he had gotten to look upon as his mother. He wrote her a letter full of affection, told her that he was praying that her health would be restored, gave her lots of spiritual advice and finally, in the case that God would call her to Him, asked her to pray that he would have "a great spirit of sacrifice and prayer in keeping with his vocation."

Let us quote another letter, one to his father, after a long period of silence and therefore more delicate:

> Father, please forgive my silence. Actually I have nothing to write except what it is good for me to repeat: the assurance of my affection for you. That is the way affection goes: it has only one thing to say, always the same. That is especially true at La Trappe. Here, in fact, one has an image of eternity. Time passes, and yet nothing changes. I remain always the same, both physically and morally. I do not lack things to do, and above all there is the charm of the cloistered life. My letters are short and rare because my time is taken up. But there is no end to the filial and fraternal affection that I have for all of you.

Another charming letter to his father dates from June, 1906:

> Don't worry about me. I am putting up with my exile joyfully, and have little desire to allay it by visits. But you can come when you would like, you will find your son full of joy to welcome you. You will even find lodging and your meals in the monastery. It would be charming for these Belgians to see a true Breton from Brittany. If ever you do come, you must come dressed as a Breton.

This same year, 1906, Brother Anselme wrote his father a letter full of allusions to the religious persecution which was raging in France:

> My personal role, as someone who lives in a free country and in the peace of the cloister, is to bring words of encouragement to you who are under a regime of persecution. It is true that it is easy to use fine words, whereas it is more difficult to act as

> one should. All the same, it seems to me that impending evil fortifies one's courage, and combat makes for generosity. It must be hard to see one's gifts and sacrifices fall into the hands of strangers. But what you have given, you have given to God. But I hope that you will still retain the use of your church. I think of the sad plight of our priests. I beg you to tell them that I sympathize with them, and also give them my wishes for saintly courage to face the coming year.

Deep down in his heart the monk Anselme felt a bit ashamed that he was not sharing with his people the present disaster. "But my exile is certainly more useful to my country than my presence would be," he added, rightfully no doubt, and with tenderness.

13

Good books rather than bad pears

We have seen by his correspondence with his family during his novitiate that Brother Anselme did not hide the ascetical aspects of the Trappist life, which besides did not surprise him because he had foreseen them. There was, however, one aspect of ascesis which he discovered that disconcerted him: how little attention La Trappe attributed to intellectual curiosity and serious applied study.

> But where is study? And where are curious books to dig into? Where is the charm of following the capriciousness of the mind? Nothing like that here!

He claimed that he could endure well enough and even see the value of the practices of the Rule; but for him, who when he was with the Spiritans could follow his natural inclination for study, these ascetical practices were nothing compared to mortification of the mind. "This Rule occupies you completely; every minute and all your gestures are foreseen by the rule to the smallest detail. *That* is the biggest mortification: not having time to think."

Things lasted this way during the novitiate, and even after his first vows in 1906, when he resumed the studies he had been unable to finish as a scholastic at Chevilly, he did not say a word about the time he should normally be consecrating to his dear books. On the contrary, he spoke of nothing but fruit trees, not without humor showing some disillusion.

> I plant, I prune, I tear out. There is no lack of work. All the walls of the monastery buildings are covered with fruit trees attached to trellises: pear trees, apple trees and vines. That makes about 500 meters long, with an average of five meters high. Then there are the orchards. Lots of wood, too, and very little fruit; bad fruit due to poor soil and bad exposure. So the pears—excellent elsewhere,—are more than ordinary here. But I am neither the master or the proprietor, so I am not attached to this preoccupation. Besides, the charm of the Trappist life is to detach oneself from earthly things and learn well to seek the Only thing necessary. I am at my tenth trade: you can imagine whether I have learned even one of them correctly. So I continue to think that I would prefer good books to bad pears.

It would seem that monasteries where a Cistercian and Trappist mentality existed had more difficulty determining the place of study in their life than the Benedictine, Cluniac, Maurist and other congregations did. In his work *An Initiation to the monastic authors of the Middle Ages: The Love of Letters and the Desire for God*, Dom Jean Leclercq approached this problem with finesse, and it would not do him justice to try to summarize here in a few catchwords what he wrote. We can at least point out that the Trappist milieu in the time of Brother Anselme Le Bail was still influenced by Rancé and de Lestrange, and that it was particularly sensitive to one single aspect of the problem: that the intellectual activity of a monk risks inflating his "ego" ("*scientia inflat*")—this notorious me of self-will which Saint Benedict was a tenacious persecutor of—and that abstract knowledge can divert the monk from the necessity of personal and loving spiritual experience. The other aspect of the problem consists in asking oneself if the spiritual experience of the monk, when deprived of theological study, does not deteriorate into pure subjectivity or strict observance, which are perhaps more subtle forms of self-will. Actually, if theological knowledge can in fact "puff the monk up," it can equally be a path of objective obedience to divine Revelation and the Tradition of the Fathers. Yesterday there were deviations, and today there still are, in both of these directions. We know that, in the past, just as in our time, syntheses and ways to reconcile the two approaches are fortunately possible and fruitful. Let us permit Dom Leclercq—and by him, Saint Bernard—teach us daring and wisdom in this matter.

> Freedom of the spirit alone enables the mystical author to use his literary gifts with this degree of liberty. Carried to extremity this freedom and this poverty would result in silence, for experience is a form of intimate love exchanged between the soul and God; in what is personal and incommunicable it is predisposed to silence. But this same charity assumes another aspect in that, besides the mystic, it includes his neighbor. If the mystic is a shepherd of souls, a doctor and a writer of the Church, he has the duty to communicate to others what he knows about God. And if he speaks of this, he should do it well since whatever he says will always be imperfect. Saint Bernard thinks the angels will help him. Since they also are servants of the word, they "administer" to the mind the beautiful conceptions and images which make them perceptible. But while images express God they likewise conceal Him. This radical imperfection in everything the mystic tries to express succeeds in detaching him from his literary pursuits and does away with any self-satisfaction he might take in what he writes. Literature, he knows, with all its formalities and necessary laws is an example of the powerlessness of our condition, its limitations and the inadequacy of what we say to represent what gives us our life. To become aware of this lack and this impediment is to intensify one's desire to possess God fully in eternity.
>
> At the extreme frontiers of literature, therefore, the whole realm of the ineffable opens out. At this point the word must yield before the inexpressible gifts accorded by God's liberty and liberality. In the last of his completed sermons on the *Song of Songs*, Saint Bernard stressed this truth in a text which is at it were his literary testament:
>
>> And now someone may perhaps ask me what it means to enjoy the Word. I shall answer him: Seek out, rather, someone who has had this experience and ask him. For if it had been given to me—even to such as me—to have that experience, do you think that I could express the inexpressible? Listen to the Apostle Saint Paul who did

> have this experience: "If we seemed out of our senses, it was for God; but if we are being reasonable now, it is for your sake" (2 Co 5.13). In other words, when I am all alone with God it is very different than when I am with you. What takes place between God and me I can experience but cannot express; whereas when I am with you I try to speak in a way so that you will understand.

In 1924 Dom Anselme would take a position on this problem that was as audacious as it was circumspect. He explained it in his work: *L'Ordre de Cîteaux. La Trappe*, at the end of chapter 5: "The particular goal of knowledge in the Cistercian Order." We will come back to this later, more amply. At that time, in 1912, scarcely eight years after he entered La Trappe, Brother Anselme still had only timid intuitions on this subject. In a letter to his family, however, he was already audacious:

> Hay-making, harvest, reaping . . . Here's something about the material side which can no doubt be of interest to you. As for me, I can scarcely take any interest in it. I work quite hard loading and unloading hay and I do, of course, find a certain pleasure in hard work. But to occupy myself with the question of interests, success, quality, value, that sort of thing doesn't attract me. And, in this respect, I remain what I was before. The intellectual side of life has always interested me more and when I became a monk-laborer I did not cease to be a bookman. Moreover, this is more suitable for a monk, because his life is the life of the soul, and not that of a workman who earns 3,50 francs a day in Belgium.

14

When the will of God pursues you

Scarcely after being ordained a priest on August 24, 1909, and until October 1913 when he was elected abbot, Father Anselme had a series of responsibilities fall on him; he accepted them only because he saw God's will there. While already secretary of his abbot Dom Norbert, he was made Master of the Lay Brothers. He took the accomplishment of this charge seriously, as the following two examples show.

The first manifestation of this seriousness was his prayer for "his" Lay Brothers. A secret prayer, we would know nothing about it if Dom Anselme's personal notebooks had not been preserved. There, day after day and for years he wrote down in detail, in four columns, when and for whom he celebrated his daily Mass. The fourth column, entitled "*Cogitate quod agitis*," which means "Think of the Mystery you are celebrating," reveals to us the communion of prayer and friendship which he established with his Lay Brothers.

> Mass for my Lay Brothers: "Watch over them, O Mary. Be their Mother and their Doctor." For my Lay Brothers: "O Mary, may each of them be completely yours." For my Lay Brothers: "Father, may they come to you by Christ, and to Christ by Mary." For my Lay Brothers: "You, too, go to my vineyard, and I will give you what you deserve, in all justice." For my Lay Brothers: "May they rejoice in their weaknesses and put their strength in you, Lord." Mass for my Lay Brothers: "The time is coming when the true adorers of my Father will adore him is spirit and in truth."

The list is long. As one continues to look through it one discovers there, with some emotion, the tender affection Father Anselme had for his brothers who were simple and fragile, of course, but true adorers of the Father in spirit and privileged sons of the Virgin Mary. In fact, were the Lay Brothers not committed to saying the rosary rather than the Psalter which the monks chanted in choir?

It is precisely here that we come upon the second evidence of the seriousness that Father Anselme attached to his responsibility as Master of Lay Brothers: he wanted to give the religious status of his dear Lay Brothers its proper worth, and by doing so give liturgical and ecclesial value to the office they recited together. Without any trace of being a champion of a cause, but simply by his spirit of faith and his theological soundness, Father Anselme had in 1909 a point of view which was not different from that of the Second Vatican Council sixty years later, when it gave to the People of God, as well as to priests and monks, the responsibility for assuming the liturgical prayer of the Church, with simply the form of the Liturgical Hours being susceptible to adaptation to different states of life.

So it was that this attentive Master of Lay Brothers composed a small book of a hundred pages for them, an authentic initiation to the grandeur of their status and to the ecclesiastical significance of their prayer. The Introduction reads as follows:

> Undoubtedly, one cannot claim canonically that the Office of the Lay Brothers is the public Prayer of the Church. Nevertheless, there are so many reasons that can be given which proclaim the grandeur of their official prayer and, at the same time, of their state!
>
> True religious they are, and by this title alone their life is already dedicated to God. *A fortiori*, their prayer Office is a cult offered to God. But more specifically than in other religious Congregations, the Cistercian Lay Brothers are "vowed to divine Cult" by established practice in our Order. By their very institution the Lay Brothers are coadjutors of the canonical Office in order to permit the choir monks to fulfill this obligation. Our Cistercian tradition specifically affirms that the choir

> monks accept Lay Brothers, without whom they could not fulfill the Divine Office day and night .
>
> Consequently, strictly speaking the Lay Brothers form a part of an Order devoted to the liturgical Office. So they participate very intimately in the merits of this solemn praise which the entire monastic community renders to God by the voices of the choir monks.

These remarks may seem somewhat out of date today, when monastic communities no longer make a distinction between choir monks and lay brothers. Yet the temptation may still persist in a community to distinguish, or even to oppose, the monks who are more available for prayer in choir and those who are more taken up with material, economic or pastoral tasks.

And doesn't there still exist in the Church a tenacious temptation to distinguish, or even oppose, a monastic elite and the "*Vulgum pecus*" of the laity? Father Anselme concluded his introduction to "The Excellence of the Lay Brothers' Office" by a quotation from Aelred of Rievaulx which applies to every ecclesial community, yesterday and today:

> Each one should consider whatever he has as belonging to all his brothers. What belongs to a family belongs to each one . . . Let the lay brothers not bewail that they do not sing or watch as much as the monks. Nor the monks, that they do not work as much as the lay brothers. For in very truth I say: whatever one does belongs to the whole community, just as what belongs to the community belongs to each one. For we are all one body in Christ, and we are each one a member of the others (Sermon 3 for the Feast of Saint Benedict 10-11).

In 1911, it was with regret that he left his dear Lay Brothers to assume another responsibility: that of Master of the Choir Novices. The day after he assumed this assignment he continued his Mass intentions "*pro meis novitiis*" (for my novices) which until that time he had offered "*pro meis conversis*" (for my Lay Brothers).

> Mass for my novices: "O Mary, be their master: teach them, lead them, give them ardour." For my novices: "May I be, in the desert, a voice which calls them." For my novices: "O Mother, their guide, give them fervor." For my novices: "Help us to contemplate Jesus." For my novices: "Give my sons knowledge of and a taste for Holy Scripture." Mass for my novices: "O holy Mary, without you I can do nothing for them. They are yours: conform them to Jesus."

Just as for his Lay Brothers, the list of Dom Anselme's prayers for his novices is long. One looks through it with the same emotion and with the same admiration for this monk who, far from attracting the novices to himself, confides them to the hands of Mary and her divine Son.

The human and spiritual quality of these young choir novices was of course not necessarily better than that of the Lay Brothers, but from that year on Father Anselme applied his attention to the intellectual formation they needed for the Divine Office in choir and for the priesthood, as well as for responsibilities they might be called upon to assume in the future. He adhered to it with tenacious conviction during his whole life by the elaboration and effective implementation of a plan for serious methodical and continuous studies. In fact, already in 1911 he understood very clearly and practiced very conscientiously what he wrote in 1924, in his previously mentioned work, *L'Ordre de Cîteaux. La Trappe*:

> Formation to the religious life is basically "one," just as religious life itself is. And yet, in practice, religious life takes on the form of its exterior framework: thoughts and aspirations vary according to each Institute. So formation should be geared to this end; and formation for the Cistercian life should consequently be distinctly Cistercian. Teaching sometimes seems very hard during the two years of the novitiate: the program is so full.
>
> First of all, it includes "asceticism." The manual for this teaching should be the Rule of Saint Benedict. One cannot imagine how anyone who hopes to make profession according

> to this legislation could choose another guide to prepare himself for it. This Rule, in fact, is not only a disciplinary code; it is a sure guide for the spiritual life. Although it prescribes rules for the exterior life, it is much more in view of forming the soul; and to do that it indicates the foundation to build upon, the method to follow and the summit to attain. The Rule of Saint Benedict, explained by the novice master in the context of a developed commentary, is the perfect manual of monastic ascesis.

What is obvious to us today was not so in certain Trappist monasteries at that time, when the Rule of Saint Benedict was looked upon especially as a disciplinary code to which were added the sacrosanct Usages and Customs. The spirituality was taken preferably from works such as *The Imitation of Jesus Christ* and manuals which "uplifted the soul." Thomas Merton brought this out in his book *The Waters of Siloe*:

> At a time when, in the Cistercian Order, the Rule of Saint Benedict was scarcely thought of as a manual for formation, Dom Le Bail penetrated far into the theology of the Cistercian writers of the twelfth century. Taking them as his commentators on the Rule of Saint Benedict, he had evolved a clear and well-ordered spiritual doctrine, by the light of which he was able to give his novices a thoroughly Cistercian intellectual formation. . . .[1]

This spirit of balance and spiritual healthiness, of simplicity and clarity was also communicated by Father Anselme, to a certain degree and not without labor, to the Cistercian Order of the Strict Observance. If he was solicitous about getting the young monks interested in serious studies in the monastery, and even outside the cloister in universities, it was above all so that they might attain human development, which he believed to be preliminary to the monastic life. He drew up his teaching, which he took from the Rule of Saint Benedict or from Saint Bernard's

[1] Thomas Merton, *The Water of Siloe* (New York: Harcourt Brace and Co., 1949) 192.

school of charity, while putting it into practice. If he was a pioneer in many areas, and even if he is outdated today, one can see his influence—along with others—in his cherished community of Scourmont which he had prepared for all the changes that would take place later.

Hundreds of papers—if not a thousand—have been preserved on which continually reworked commentaries on the Rule follow one another and become more and more perceptive. Sometimes using black ink, sometimes red, Fr. Anselme dissected and put in order the chapters and verses, and then arranged them in synoptic tables. He sometimes accomplished a real *tour de force* which probably would have astonished Saint Benedict himself; and we could no doubt find some things that are arbitrary. But taken as a whole his presentation is reliable, enlightening and, in any case, well-structured for beginners in the spiritual art. This meticulous and laborious research on the Rule is proportionate to Fr. Anselme's conviction that the Benedictine Rule is the guide for the spiritual life of every Cistercian.

Besides study of the Rule, the Novice Master assigned to his novices study of the Psalms as their primordial work as young Cistercians, a work which he rightly said had been encouraged throughout the whole of ancient monasticism. Once again, joining a gesture to his words and practice to his idea, he took up his pen and has left us numerous handwritten pages where the principal psalms of the Office are commented on verse by verse, not only by Saint Bernard but also by unpublished writers such as Henry of Marsy, Baldwin of Ford, Aelred, John of Belesnes, Thomas the Cistercian, Joachim of Flores, John of Limoges and others.

The Psalter, he wrote, is the prayer book of the monk, the book for all ages of the monastic life. Furthermore, it becomes—according to Saint Bernard's comparison—rain producing fruit for the soul only after it has been the object of continual rumination. It then becomes also a source of joy: "You will not lack rain from heaven; I mean to say: devotion in prayer, the pleasant rumination of the Psalms, the consolation coming from Scripture."

And this is the third work of novices: study of Holy Scripture, the Bible which is, more than any other book, "the" book of the monk, which Saint Jerome advises us never to let out of our hands.

Still, there is a monastic way of reading Scripture, and for that the Cistercian monk should take his Father Saint Bernard as model, realizing that the effect produced by Holy Scripture in this great monk of Cîteaux can be brought about also in himself. In *L'Ordre de Cîteaux. La Trappe*, Dom Le Bail spoke quite a lot about this.

First of all, he referred to a passage from the "*Vita sancti Bernardi.*" This was followed by an extract from a letter written by Saint Bernard to a contemporary who was a master in Holy Scripture:

> Saint Bernard quoted Scripture so pertinently and with such ease that one would not believe that he was following the text, but that he himself was followed by it and that he bent it as he wished, so forcefully was he guided by the Spirit who inspired these texts. The Lord had filled him with the spirit of wisdom and intelligence so that he could "explore the sources of rivers, and bring to daylight secrets that were hidden" (Jb 28.11). He himself once admitted that while he was meditating or praying he had seen the whole of Scripture placed at his feet, so to speak, and unveiled before his eyes.

All this knowledge of Scripture, continued Dom Anselme, had as its single and immediate goal to keep divine love alive in the soul . . .

> Saint Bernard himself told his monks what they should seek in Scripture. He explained this to a master in Holy Scripture who sought there what our blessed Father did not judge was suitable for a monk: "You, my brother, who read the prophets and who no doubt believe that you understand their writings, you will surely recognize that Christ in person is the meaning of the prophecies. So if it is he that you are ardently eager to possess, I assure you that you will reach him much sooner if you start following him instead of going ahead with your reading. Why seek the Word in books when we have him so near to us in his flesh? It is a long time since he left the dim reclusion

> of the prophets to show himself to the eyes of sinners, and since he came down from the cloudy and dark heights of the ancient law like a young bridegroom from his wedding bed, to dart forth in the vast plains of the Gospel. We need only our own ears to hear Himself crying out in his temple: 'If any man is thirsty, let him come to me and drink' (Jn 7:37-38) or 'Come to me, all you who labor and are overburdened, and I will refresh you' (Mt 11:28). Would you be afraid of collapsing from exhaustion, where Truth himself promises to strengthen you? If you have so much pleasure in drinking the muddy water of the wells fed by the rain from heaven, you will find the water that you will draw from the clear fountain of the Saviour much more pleasant.
>
> Oh! If only you may one day taste—even if it would be just one morsel—this exquisite bread by which Jerusalem is satisfied. . . . How happy I would then be to see you finally with me in the school of Christ, and to support by my hands the purified urn of your heart, so that he may fill it with this divine unction which communicates all knowledge! How I would like to break with you the bread still piping hot, just out of the oven as they say, this bread which Christ lavishly distributes so often to his poor with heavenly generosity!"

Dom Le Bail thought that in his efforts to assimilate the Sacred Books the monk can—and always following Saint Bernard's example—sometimes prefer the text without any commentary. One of Bernard's biographers related in fact "that there was no explanation which helped him to understand the Word of God as well as the Word itself; and that as for all the truths and meanings he saw shining there, it was rather at the source itself of Holy Scripture that he found and tasted them, rather than in the little streams of the commentaries."

Still, being suspicious of intellectual laziness and too invasive subjectivity Dom Anselme was careful to point out that the monk should always be careful to rely on the pillars of the Church: the Fathers, who commented on Scripture the way Saint Bernard did. One of his biographers said, in fact: "He was not less humble when reading the works of commentators of Holy Scripture recommended for their holiness and their orthodoxy. Without claiming to put the meanings he himself discovered on the same level as theirs, but rather walking faithful in their footsteps, he himself often went to drink at the same source as they had."

To those of his fellow Trappist monks who regularly made the objection that *scientia inflat*, "knowledge puffs one up with pride," referring textually to the "*Vita Sancti Bernardi*," Dom Anselme affirmed that, for a monk, studying the Tradition is a way of practicing humility ("*humiliter legens*"), refusing the pretension to take his own sensibility as his only point of reference ("*nequaquam eorum sensibus suos sensus aequabat*"), submitting to the Fathers ("*subjiciebat*") and being faithful to a path that has already been traced out ("*vestigiis eorum fideliter inhaerens*").

The Novice Master Anselme, however, was not preoccupied only with the intellectual formation of his novices. He also inculcated in them "refinement of conscience," such as he described it in a letter to his aunt:

> It is an inclination of the soul which very quickly makes it conscious of what is contrary to or less in conformity with the will of God; and as soon as the soul feels this in itself, it places itself in the presence of God and prays Him to give it the strength to triumph over all temptations. This soul does not make a distinction between little sins and big sins, because all sins should be avoided. To arrive at this point it is necessary to be recollected, because in the midst of noise and dissipation a person does not hear this interior voice which tells one what is good and what is bad, and consequently one commits a lot of faults and does not advance in holiness.

He made his own examination of conscience in the same letter:

> A life of prayer is made easier by silence and the hidden life. But I have not gotten there yet. Still, I would not like to be a Carthusian, because the common life at La Trappe is more crucifying. The Carthusian has his own private place where he is the master. The Trappist is always at the mercy of his neighbor. I do not desire death either, to tell you the truth; rather,

> I fear it. But I recognize this fact: in this life, one always remains pitiable, time does not cure anything. So it would seem that it is preferable to go to heaven, where one no longer offends God. But I patiently await God's time, perhaps too patiently.

In another letter to his aunt, so dear to him, he communicated his enthusiasm for the liturgical life, just as he communicated it to his novices:

> These liturgical customs are not a spiritual luxury. This is simply the Christian life, like every baptized person should live it under the direction of the Church. When one lives one's own little pious life, alone in one's nook, one is not sure of doing what is best, and then, in any case, one is alone. With the Church, on the contrary, it is the Holy Spirit who directs the sanctification of souls in an infallible way, and this comes about when people are together, as in a family. I understand more and more that the direction the Church gives is more valuable in the work of sanctification than following one's little personal plan. This is because one's little personal plan, even with a director, is often false, and in any case always limited. The plan of the Church is as vast as God's plan, and as infallible as the Holy Spirit. . . .
>
> The celebration of the Office is union with Jesus in his role as Mediator. Jesus, the Word incarnate, has as mission to praise his Father, to adore Him, to thank Him, to ask his pardon and help for human beings. And in this office of mediation, He does not want to be alone. It is good to understand that, to get free from oneself and to be united to Jesus' interests, to be preoccupied with his work. Saint Benedict called his work "the work of God" ("*Opus Dei*"), in the sense that it is labor in God's service; and furthermore the monk is called God's workman ("*Quaerens Dominus operarium suum*"): God seeks his man for work in the prayer of the Church.

Briefly, in the formation which Father Master Anselme gave to his choir novices from 1911 on, everything was in place: study of the Rule of Saint Benedict as guide for the spiritual life of the monk; study of the Psalter as continual rumination by the Cistercian monk; study of Holy Scripture in Saint Bernard's savory way and in the orthodox manner of the Church Fathers; vigilance in loving refinement of one's own conscience; immersion in liturgical prayer, in communion with Christ the Mediator.

In April, 1913, Father Anselme received a new sign of confidence from his Abbot: he was appointed Prior. As such, he became more and more the right hand of his Abbot, Dom Norbert. Then after the General Chapter that year, Dom Norbert, who had been made Procurator of the Order at Rome, had his Prior read to the community of Scourmont his act of resignation as Abbot. Those who were present when this took place said that Father Anselm's voice trembled with emotion: Was it because of his tenderness as a son and very dear friend who was losing such valuable support? Was it because of his intuition that led him to foresee and dread that he would become his successor as Abbot?

Beauty, creating things
Do you foresee their fragility?
If you know it, why roses,
Why life and this summer?

They are to die in an instant
Of their beauty received, offered,
In I know not what: Time?
Pure splendor and pure loss.

And God said: "The soul has its beauty
In knowing it is unsatisfied,
Only its desire for the infinite,
By its torment, makes it perfect."

C. D.

15

Who is the man who wishes to see happy days?

By 1913 Father Anselme had already lived in the cloister at Scourmont for several years. He had been Master of the Lay Brothers, Sub-Prior, Master of Choir Novices, and was about to become Prior. It is impossible to imagine that this man, so honest as he was, had not evolved positively and had not, as was his habit, left written traces of what he had become. Thanks to letters which he wrote to members of his family, we can in fact have a good idea of this man who was thirty-five years old and had nine years of experience in the monastic life.

> I relish more and more the beauty of the religious life. Isn't that curious? The most austere life, the most deprived of what people call the pleasures of the world, becomes, if it is accepted voluntarily, the life the most sure and fruitful for happiness here below. I have meditated with my novices on this question found in Psalm 33, and repeated by Saint Benedict in the Prologue of his Rule: "*Quis est homo qui vult vitam et cupit videre dies bonos.*" ("Does someone yearn for life and desire to see good days?") We all experience this happiness here in the cloister; and people who visit us, especially those who live with us for several days, feel it. It is no doubt a proof that happiness is not found in subservience to matter, but in detachment with regard to it. To accomplish God's will at every instant, and in doing so to renounce our own desires, that is the secret of our happy life.

Faithful to his leaning for introspection, Father Anselme reflected on his own life:

> At the beginning, when one struggles at La Trappe, one works there like someone condemned to forced labor. Not that one goes at it unwillingly; but one has no horizons. One simply thinks that he has come to La Trappe to save his soul and do penance; and says to oneself that the sooner it will be over the better. This is still egotistical, even though it is spiritual.
>
> But with time, experience, reflection and purification of the heart, we discover that God has thrust us into La Trappe to be the first to accept the mercy that God wants to offer to all sinners on earth. It is up to the Trappists to do that, singing God's gifts night and day, while their missionary brothers teach, correct and direct souls throughout the world. That way, each one is contented with his lot, convinced that he is working for God's kingdom in the world.

This apostolic and ecclesial dimension of a Trappist's life is obvious to us today, but it was not so at that time. In our time we are more sensitive to the fact that different vocations are complementary and to the interaction of charisms. Father Anselme already foresaw this:

> How beautiful our life as a monk is! It is no longer the drab commonplace life of the Trappist that one hears about usually: not to sleep, not to eat, not to speak, always not . . . Our life is positive, love, communion with Jesus who sacrificed himself on Calvary for the salvation of all human beings. I want to be a good monk for the consolation of the world.

16

Confidence: I will show you that I am a father

On October 4, 1913, after a regular vote, Father Anselme was elected Abbot of Scourmont, the fourth "since the foundation." Dom Bonaventure De Groote, Abbot of Saint-Sixte and Father Immediate, presided the election and "*feliciter*" confirmed it with "joyful satisfaction." He, just as many other people, had no doubt foreseen whom the community would choose, because the day before the election he received a letter from Chévilly-par-L'Hay (Seine), dated October 1, which was a reply to a question he himself had put to the Superior of the Spiritan Fathers the week before. Mail service was slow in those days!

> I am very happy to give you an excellent recommendation concerning Brother Emmanuel Le Bail, former scholastic in our institute, and now a professed religious of your Order. All the memories his superiors and fellow seminarians have of him are excellent, full of esteem and edification. He entered our institute with very good credentials in September, 1898, and made his first temporary vows in October of the next year, after completing his novitiate in a way that was entirely satisfactory to his superiors. When his first vows expired in 1903 and he was once again entirely free, he withdrew from the community in a way that was fully in keeping with the rule, and perfectly honorable. Our only regret was that we lost a good candidate whom God was calling to another Order. To our knowledge there is nothing of a derogatory nature concerning the excellence of his reputation, or which would diminish the confidence that one can have in him. We are very happy and not at

> all surprised that this Father is being considered for a higher position. We would be the first to rejoice about it before God.
>
> Please accept, Reverend Father Abbot, my very respectful sentiments.
>
> Signed: Father Berthet, Director. Countersigned with the seal of the Congregation of the Holy Spirit and the Holy Heart of Mary.

This recommendation could not be more clear; besides that, it is written perfectly, with no clumsy blunders. How did this letter find its way into Dom Anselme's files? That's a mystery. It might have been by secret connivance between Dom Anselme and Dom Bonaventure: a fraternal way of encouraging and pacifying the newly-elected abbot. The Spiritan Father's phrase: "We are very happy and not at all surprised" is the leitmotif in the copious correspondence which the new abbot received between October 4, the date of his election, and October 24, the date of his blessing. This absence of surprise was shown principally in the Cistercian milieu, by Abbots who had spent some time at Scourmont, and by a certain number of Trappists who had lived their first years at Scourmont but later made their stability in another monastery. It would be tedious to quote here the phrases—necessarily more or less similar—which told Dom Anselme that his election was not surprising. Besides that, these letters were always very personal and not simply according to protocol or courtesy. Numerous letters brought out the evident bond of friendship that existed between Dom Norbert and Dom Anselme, which was a sign of promise for the future. From these letters we have chosen, because of its particularly amusing style, a passage written by a monk of Cîteaux:

> My very Reverend Father, it was a very pleasing joy for me to learn of your election as abbot. My predictions and prophecies have been abundantly fulfilled. May God, who does all things well, be a thousand and one times blessed! I say "my prophecies," because when I came back to Cîteaux on September 23 I said to the Porter, who told me that Dom Norbert had been chosen as Procurator General: "Oh, his successor at Chimay is already chosen; it will without any doubt be my former Father

> Master, who is at present Prior." In early October I said the same thing in a letter I wrote to Father Baudelle, the vicar at Tourcoing. So I recognize clearly that I have been a prophet at least once in my life. But I imagine that in this case, a lot of other people have been prophets like me. So I am happy, very happy.

More touching were the letters that the new Abbot received from some of the lay brothers of his community, in scrunched up and clumsy writing on both sides of little sheets of square-block paper. Here we discover to what point their former Master of Lay Brothers had gained their love.

> My Reverend Father, I promise you obedience until death. I protest (sic) that I want to be like soft wax in your hands, I want to take your spirit and do everything that you expect of me, with all the ardor, good will and complete devotion of a son. I want to be yours just like I want to belong to Jesus and the Blessed Virgin, since from now on you are their representative among us. I do not know how to explain to you what is in my heart, but I hope that the Blessed Virgin will help you to guess it. All I can say to you is that I am even more your child than ever, that it is you who will direct me toward God even more paternally and directly than in the past. I ask your pardon with all my might for all the grief I have caused you by attachment to my own ideas and my personal opinions. Now, for all my life, I no longer want to think of anything but to obey, in everything, completely, for the love of God. And I want to thank you today—I hope you will permit me to do so—for all the good that you have done me. God has used you to make me better: I am grateful to you for that, right to the bottom of my soul. But especially, and it is especially this that I want to tell you from my heart: I thank you for giving me to the Blessed Virgin. I feel that I love her so much now. When we will be in heaven, I will still come to thank you for her.

And this note from another Lay Brother:

> My very dear Father, I have as it were a secret presentiment that your soul is fearful and anguished before the perspective of the account you will have to render on the terrible Day. That

> is why I would like to be able to find in my filial heart some good word which might be able to pacify your chagrin. First of all, it is certain that if you have great confidence in Jesus, He Himself will make up for what you won't do. Yesterday morning I served the Mass of the Sacred Heart, and I prayed a lot to the Heart of Jesus that you may be his own Abbot, counting only on Him and entrusting to his care to fulfill all the obligations of your charge, or rather to make them perfect. For the graces you will need for the direction of souls, you can count on the prayers of the Church on the day of your blessing. I have already read them; they are admirable. Besides that, everybody seems to be very happy about your election. So you can count on general good will. For my part, and insofar as I am able, I will lighten your burden by always being ready to carry out your desires.

The rest of this note is quite astonishing, because the lay brother who wrote it continued by spelling out concretely his concern about helping his new Abbot in several areas. He expressed himself courageously:

> First of all, dear Father Abbot, if it suits you better to relieve me of my post as sub-cellarer, don't be afraid to do so. That won't insult me. In the past that would have been hard for me, because I had hoped to do some good. But finally I was disappointed because my good intentions were thwarted at every moment by the Father Cellarer who was always preaching about material work. Because of that I was reduced to the conclusion that the greatest good I can do as a lay brother is indirectly by prayer and intention, which one can do more easily in humble jobs.
>
> Next, for your own good I would like to point out to you a fault you have. One would like a little more unction in your teaching. One finds your instructions tiring, because of the numerous divisions and subdivisions. But I suppose you wouldn't know how to do any differently.
>
> Finally, it is the time to remind you of what Saint Theresa of the Child Jesus said about the poison of praise that those who accept the first place get every day. And she adds that a person has to be really dead to self-love in order not to be damaged by it.

We think spontaneously of the verse of the Psalm: *"Love and truth embrace."* And we can guess at Dom Anselme's joy, he who had begun and would continue his task of making his monks adults and responsible men by means of mature humility and obedience according to the Gospel of the Son of God. On the day of his blessing as abbot he no doubt received from his lay brothers a type of consolation which other congratulations and best wishes, inevitably a bit worldly, could not give him.

From outside the Cistercian milieu he received many other letters: from his family, from former fellow-students at the Minor Seminary at Sainte-Anne d'Auray, from eminent members of the clergy and, of course, from the Prince of Chimay, who attended the abbatial blessing presided by Mgr. Walravens, bishop of Tournai. We were not able to find a list of the distinguished persons who were present with Dom Anselme on October 24, the day of his blessing. Apparently there were quite a lot of people all day long and even a good number who spent the night at the guesthouse. Foreseeing over-capacity in the guesthouse, Dom Simon, Abbot of the Trappist monastery at Tilburg, Holland, wrote:

> My dear Reverend Father, do not forget that I am one of the family, and if there will be no room in the guesthouse, don't forget that I slept in the dormitory for snorers for twelve years. I could very well sleep there one more night: such nice music! Don't worry about choosing a place for me among the prelates; I repeat: being one of the family, I don't count on it, and you can do with me whatever you like! Ah! The beer . . . I just thought about it at this moment, and I am going to run to the brewery to give my order. I am sending you 8 25-liter casks express, leaving to your care to put them in the most cool place in the monastery as soon as they arrive. If the thirst of your community is not satisfied by these 8 casks, then . . . that's too bad. May the angels of the Abbey of Chimay watch over you, my dear Reverend Father. P. S. Don't forget a photographer!

And it is certainly true that it was a festive occasion, this October 24 at Scourmont. When Dom Alexis Presse was elected abbot in 1925,—that is, twelve years after his own election—Dom

Anselme was still full of joy when he thought about the atmosphere he had introduced:

> At the time of my abbatial blessing, I had the audacity to do something I have never seen repeated elsewhere, and nevertheless I am still convinced that my gesture was a good one: we had the banquet in community and not in the guesthouse. The community had their places there, making up an important number of those who were at table. In other words, those who were invited from outside the community were received in the monks' refectory and welcomed by the community of monks.

The menu was in keeping with the festivities: *potage à la Chantilly, bouchée à la Reine* (small patties), *brochet à la Hollandaise, vives frites à la macédoine,* lobster salad, crisp little cakes, fruits and desserts. In the middle of the meal Dom Le Bail rose and made the customary toast, non-conventional, as one may guess:

> Monsignor, Very Reverend Fathers, Gentlemen, my brothers, thank you, thank you! Thank you for the kind words you have just addressed to me. Thank you for your being present. Thank you for all the trimmings. In fact, for someone who embarks upon spiritual responsibility it is consoling to receive this encouragement by your tokens of honor and affection. Our Lord Jesus Christ himself accepted it (encouragement) when he went forth toward his sorrowful passion on Palm Sunday. He continues to be carried in the person of his representatives, his vicars on earth: it is the triumph before the cross, it is joy before sorrow. Thank you. Thank You. But how can I thank you worthily, my honorable guests? How will the abbot and community of Saint-Joseph pay their debt of gratitude? Oh, I have quickly found the means to do so! By promising to be what we should be, and by continuing to give what we should give. We are in the Church of Tournai, in the region of Chimay. What should we be and what do we want to be in this Church? What contemplatives should be in the universal Church: the heart. In the mystical Body of the Church, contemplatives should fulfill the functions that the heart fulfills in the human body: it gives life to the body, warms it and enlivens all the other members.

> So with gratitude I offer you the tribute of the heart: love and devotion.
>
> Love and devotion to you, Monsignor and Father of this Church of Tournai. Repeating the expression just taken from your wishes for our community, we promise to be the "pearl" of your Church, for your Grace's consolation, for the encouragement of your clergy and for the edification of souls.
>
> Love and devotion to you, Dom Bonaventure, Abbot of Saint-Sixte and our Father Immediate, and through you, to all our brothers of the Order of Cîteaux.
>
> Love and devotion to you, Reverend Father Dom Norbert, my Father, yes my own Father. It would not be appropriate for me to say in public what is deep in my heart. Like the prophet Elias, you have been taken from us, not yet for heaven, but for Rome. You have entrusted your cloak to me. The joy of a Father is to have a son. The joy of a son is to remain faithful to his Father's spirit. Like Elias, I say to you: Father, my own Father, leave me your spirit.
>
> Love and devotion to you, my blood-brothers, my Breton friends, the priests of Brittany with your long hair, all of you who are half of my heart. I lift my glass to the joy of this day, and to tomorrow's tears.

The evening of the 24th, the candles finished burning out. And the next day, as the sunlight sifted into the Chapter room, the new Abbot gave his inaugural talk. The tone was no longer festive, but more suited to the spiritual combat:

> My brothers, I have chosen as my abbatial motto: "Abba. Pater." You have conferred this name on me and you yourselves have given me paternity. Thank you. I will consequently be the Father of each one of you, without any sort of distinction. Abba, then, means Father. Have confidence: I will show you that I am a father; I will have a father's heart for all of you. As for me, I undertake my abbatial charge—not knowing what it will be like—with confidence. What I do know is that my ideal as abbot will be to maintain our family. First of all, by safeguarding full observance of the Rule of Saint Benedict, our Cistercian Usages, fasting, the Divine Office in choir, work, silence and solitude.

> In a word, the simplicity of our life. Next, by maintaining a pure and enlightened contemplative life. It will be pure if we protect ourselves from activism, either pastoral or industrial. It will be enlightened if, by being careful not to confuse devotion with interior life, we seek knowledge that is in the service of love, knowledge of God and the tradition of the Church. All that is our family heritage, a treasure; and woe to any Abbot who might ignore or waste it.
>
> Let us reap the heritage of the spirit of the second Abbot of Scourmont, Dom Godefroid Bouillon: he had a firm hand and a loving heart. I would like to inherit his firmness, to act like an Abbot since I am one. Let us reap the spirit of the third Abbot of Scourmont, Dom Norbert Sauvage who, contrary to his name, was a man of astonishing gentleness. I would like to inherit his discretion, which enabled him to find a solution to many difficulties.
>
> From you I expect filial confidence. That is the meaning of your having chosen me. I give you my affection; give me yours, without considering the simply human side of things.
>
> You and I, let us have faith. Let us travel together towards heaven.

The curtain fell: daily life was resumed. A month later, Dom Anselme wrote to his father:

> Governing souls for God, purely, always and in all things, is difficult. Often one exposes one's soul for others. So pray for me, that I may be saved and sanctified.

Dom Le Bail had taken just his first steps on the rocky path of his abbacy.

17

A combat outside the cloister: The War of 1914–1918

The first trial in store for the young abbot came suddenly. At a time when Dom Anselme was still "freshly elected" and had all the energy and audacity necessary to give new incentive to his monks for the spiritual combat in the "*acies fraterna*"—the fraternal troops according to Saint Benedict—, behold, the year 1914 brought with it the beginning of a combat that was less spiritual, the long and huge war of 1914–1918. In April, on the feast of Saint Anselme, the Father Abbot made his first examination of conscience before the community. "Have I accomplished up until now a little bit of the program that I had drawn up for myself?" he asked himself. "Yes, I think that up until now I have fulfilled fairly well the role of Abbot, *Magister et Pater*. Oh, there is still a lot to do; still, I hope to get there. I will strive to be more of a father for all of you and for each one of you."

August, 1914: the war broke out. Dom Anselme was called up along with eleven of his monks. Since this represented an impediment with regard to his abbatial responsibilities, he delegated his powers to Father Charles Perpète who governed the monastery during the whole war. As for Dom Anselme, he was to serve his country in a mobile medical unit of the sixth Army. After moving around to a number of places the unit 5-61 was stationed in a small town in the Department of Oise. From there, he wrote to his father:

> For over a month now, I am no longer sharing the dangers and sufferings of the war. When I arrived here I was very sick, very exhausted, very thin. Now everyone accuses me of not having the look and build of a warrior. Our life, in fact, is not the life of someone fighting in a war. The Germans are 20 or 30 kilometers from here; we still hear our big cannon, but nothing else. It is calm, an ordinary life like at Séglien, except that we see soldiers everywhere.

And as he liked to do, he gave a very detailed account of how he used his time during the day:

> I get up between 5:30 and 6:00, and I am the first one up. I go and say my Mass. Then I come back for breakfast: a big cup of coffee with hot milk. After that I run to close myself up (because it is freezing here and snowing) in a room that a good Breton, astray in this country, has put at the disposition of the medical unit. There, nice and warm, we write, we read and we pray. We go out for dinner, etc. Finally, we go to bed very early, on straw it is true, but we are well wrapped up in blankets. Sundays we replace the pastor of the parish. You must agree that this life does not seem much like war. I say that to our shame, because I do not like this life. I languish here, and I prefer the times when the medical unit has work to do: receiving the wounded, caring for them, showing them a lot of attention so as to touch their souls, and preparing them for death, if necessary. I had learned all that and, you see, now we have lost the habit of doing these things. That life of devoted service was more suitable to a priest and Trappist religious. One consolation while I am stationed here is to receive letters from my religious who have left for the war, like I have. We write to each other faithfully, and that is a great joy for us. Unfortunately there are two from whom I have no news, one of them is Dom Norbert. I do not know what has become of him, and I am trying as best I can to find him. About Chimay, I am almost sure that everything still remains undamaged. This whole kind of life should not make us too sad, and especially, let us remain good Christians. Let us see God's will in all this and the good which will result from it for our religion.

At the time when he wrote these lines, on November 14, he could still have some illusions about this. Alas, later on, prolonged absence from family and home, the pressure of elementary instincts, the materialistic environment and even habituation to being in danger, would lead the majority to a weakening of religious sentiments. Fr. Benoît Attout, who at that time was with Dom Anselme in Calais, remembered having tried in vain to obtain a book that was a bit interesting, something different from the newspaper with its morose war reports. In this town which was, after all, quite a big one, he had to be satisfied with being able to get at a good price a work on Old Medieval French. But the Father Abbot struggled to keep the men's minds from getting completely rusty, and by his ingenious stubbornness he succeeded in organizing a small but substantial library of spirituality for the use of the religious and priests who were mobilized.

In another letter, to his father, Dom Le Bail drew up his first spiritual account of the interior self-stripping that the war was little by little bringing about for him.

> I have all my time to meditate on the lessons of the war. For myself, being obliged to leave the cloister has not been without bearing fruit. Being called up and the change from being a monk to a soldier have made me more humble and abandoned to God's will. I was so attached to the calm atmosphere of the monastic life, I had a certain liking for my position as abbot. I dreamed about putting into practice my plans and projects so as to have a good monastery. I had already begun work on a study room which would have given my monks more taste for a meditative and studious life. It ended when the call to active service stopped the work and dispersed the monks. Perhaps right now it is in ruins. I had to sacrifice a lot of other things, too. I had a flourishing novitiate, monks destined to assume important responsibilities in the monastery; I wanted to send two of them to Rome this year. All that is at a standstill. It is the same for a lot of things which legitimately gave joy to my heart. Now I am learning to be more abandoned to the will of God. The future will be what He wills it to be. For me, this is my first lesson from this war.

> War has also this advantage for us as monks: it forces us to practice what is essential in our life in a milieu which is not ours. I am speaking not only of myself, but of my monks. We are twelve monks of Saint-Joseph's who are in the war. At present I am in contact with all of them, and I can see that all of them are profiting from the war. It is even the young ones who are profiting most. It is a joy for me to receive their letters, and to see how each one of them in his particular situation is striving to remain a monk perfectly; it is the interior life which continues in the trenches or in a hospital. They try to say the Divine Office, they give an account of the money they spend, and of their life. So even while we are away at war we form a community. All these monks, furthermore, are busy with a lot of apostolic activity. The sub-prior, for example, is in a fort. He has his chapel and organizes recitation of the rosary there. He even has soldiers who are men of the world reciting the Divine Office with him. This way, God forms us in settings which appear to be destined to deform us. It is a consolation for me to see this: it gives me more patience in supporting what cannot be avoided, and especially the long duration of the war. Our characters will be formed, we will be able to live our lives more seriously, with an upright conscience.

The last phrase of this letter is worth underlining: "For me, I will have learned to be more conciliatory, more compliant with regard to human misery." By means of the war Dom Le Bail would refine his role as Father. In January, 1915, the medical unit he was attached to moved to the Court House at Compiègne. There was much less to do, and it was less interesting there. He and two other priests formed a little community, fraternally taken in by a highly respected clergyman, Fr. Humbert, pastor of Saint-Germain. It was in his rectory that they spent most of their days, writing, reading, studying and praying. "We feel like we're a family," he wrote to his aunt; "It is even a little like the monastic life. The church is the best one in the city for its fervor and for the beauty of the chant, which is in keeping with the rules prescribed by Rome."

Toward the end of February, he again confided to his aunt:

> At a certain moment I would have almost wanted to be a medical attendant in the regiment, in order to have more occasions to practice ministry, but this wish is presumptuous and perhaps useless. Besides, when we seek to please God alone and put all our happiness in the accomplishment of His will, every situation and every condition are almost indifferent to us. So I organize my life like someone organizes his life in a stable situation. I conduct myself like someone who is fully convinced that he is going to go back to his cloister. I work for the future. I study the Rule, I am trying—even here—to complete the formation of the next Novice Master. I am thinking about all the work that is waiting for us when we will go back to Scourmont. You can see that I am not thinking about dying soon. That could happen of course, because there is still plenty of danger ahead of us. So what? In one's interior self one must be like someone whose hours are counted, but when we apply ourselves to our exterior activity we should act as though we are always going to come out alive: foresee, be prepared . . . Voilà! That's my life in the war.

This serene optimism, however, did not last. He began to feel, like a pang of hunger, the need for life in the cloister, and three times in one year he obtained permission to go to an abbey: first Sept-Fons, then the Grande-Trappe, and lastly Notre-Dame du Désert. What he wrote to his aunt about these visits sounds like it was written by a young boy, or at least by a wonder-struck novice:

> Oh! What joy! I wore my monastic habit and my abbatial insignia. I attended all the Offices and all the activities of the community, including the meals. What sweetness after exile! I needed an exile like that to make me appreciate my monastic life more, and yet, I already loved it so much. I renewed my soul as a monk and Abbot . . . What happiness to live in close contact with the Abbot of this hospitable community. I am edified, and I am learning by his example how to become a better Abbot of Scourmont . . . Everything here is a cause of joy to me: the life I have here, the family which is mine. I practice the

> common life in all points, as if I were at Chimay: getting up for vigils, office, refectory. Right off, I felt that I was in my place.

These times of renewal in the three Trappist monasteries simply made his impressions of a soldier's life more bitter, in this war which went on and on. At the end of December, 1916, he confided to his aunt:

> I feel pulled apart. I feel that this military life—because even a chaplain takes on military ways—dries up my heart. Everything becomes insipid, indifferent: family, the monastery, the spiritual life. It is a kind of sinking into what is material. Perhaps what my maternal grandmother used to say is happening to me: "When one is young, one has a young heart and is ready for action; when one gets old, the heart becomes cold like the body does." We hope that the war will end this year. So much the better. It is certainly time to go home. We are tired, materialized.

And yet, the end of the war was not near: it would take almost two more years.

1917 did not bring much change, either in the general situation or in the life of the Father Abbot. The priest who had so generously offered him hospitality in his rectory at St-Germain was transferred to the parish of St. James, the most important parish in Compiègne, where he became the archpriest. Dom Anselme followed him. The housekeeper of the new rectory was Mademoiselle Victoria, Fr. Humbert's niece, who was later remembered for her kindness and gentleness. She became the wartime godmother of all the Chimay monks who had been drafted, and welcomed them in the rectory with charming and cordial hospitality, as though it were their home. With a big heart for all the sons of the Father Abbot, the archpriest invited everyone to his table, presided over pleasant evenings before the hearth-fire and engaged the monks in high-level discussions which delighted his cultured and aristocratic mind. Whenever there was an occasion to do so, they went on excursions by bicycle to the ancient site of Royaumont or the ruins of Ourscamp Abbey. These trips were pilgrimages to their origins that Dom Anselme was particularly fond of, not simply by a taste for archaeology but, as he said, "to breathe the air sanctified by the prayer and work of our Fathers of Cîteaux."

1918: the end is near. The Germans are preparing their big spring attack. They are going to gamble everything on it, because the American troops have gotten into the battle. The German advance made it necessary to evacuate the city. The Father Abbot stopped at Senlis, thirty kilometers away. He was welcome: they had almost despaired of finding a chaplain to officiate at the many burials there. On November 13 he wrote to his niece:

> The war is over. Our normal life will begin again. I am going back to Chimay quickly. I cannot count on going to Séglien for the time being. I am anxious to see my brothers.

18

Brother, is it possible to visit the Abbey?

On November 16, an army chaplain with an impressive beard approached the porter, Brother Arnold, and in a self-assured manner and rather affected tone of voice asked him if it was possible to visit the Abbey. The brother was prompt to welcome this dignified chaplain. The farce did not last long. Alerted by the cleric's hearty laughter, the good Brother Arnold realized that this chaplain was none other than Dom Anselme whose humor had obviously not been corroded by the long war. It was also a way for him to exorcise his intense emotion.

> I am back at Chimay—he wrote to one of his brothers who was still in the army. My abbey is intact and the whole community is present. What a blessing for us from God! I arrived here November 16 after traveling for two days, not knowing anything about the situation here. Also, what a joy it was for me when I came out of the forest to see the steeple where the Belgian and French flags were flying. I went through the house several times, all alone and in silence, to taste the joy of being back here.

Still, his time of trial had not yet come to an end. Dom Anselme had to go back to Compiègne and wait to be discharged. In an attempt to obtain a three-month leave right away, he wrote to the Belgian Ambassador in Paris, explaining his motive as follows: "The head of a big enterprise desires to resume direction of it in Belgium immediately, where the French influence could be interesting." His boldness did not pay off, and he was not discharged until April, 1919. From Compiègne, he wrote to his niece about how impatient he was:

> I am weary, tired of staying here while I should be at Chimay. Here I have nothing to do but wait until I can leave. You are perhaps astonished that I am in such a hurry to run back to La Trappe. Because here, of course, things are satisfactory for me: after a good meal one can relax in a comfortable armchair, feet in front of the fire and a cigar on one's lips. Lady, what do you expect? Each person has his fancy. Mine is La Trappe, it is my home.

Dom Anselme Le Bail finished by taking his place in choir again. In the Prior's stall was Fr. Jean-Baptiste Dautrebande; in the Sub-Prior's stall, Fr. Nivard Masson; and in a privileged place, Fr. Charles Perpète, who had been an excellent administrator of the Abbey during the whole war, and whom by gratitude his Father Abbot had named honorary Prior of Notre-Dame of Saint-Joseph of Scourmont at the beginning of this new period. But who could have imagined that, twenty years later, another war would occur, a war which would be such a period of trial for the community and the world?

19

Good-bye, war! Hello, Congo!

Scarcely had the Scourmont community been delivered from the trial of war when it had to undergo another one. Theoretically this trial, unlike the one imposed upon the monks by the 1914–1918 armed conflict, was not unavoidable. It became so "*ipso facto*" because of the personality and reputation of Dom Anselme, who was called upon by the Order to undertake a formidable task. He was asked to make the canonical Visitation of the missionary-Trappists in Belgian Congo. Their Father Immediate, the Abbot of Westmalle, had the responsibility for these monks, but during the twenty-five years they had been there they had never had one single canonical visit.

In the archives of Scourmont, Westmalle and the Order, there is an impressive series of documents which deserve to be recorded in a monograph on the astounding adventure of these Trappist missionaries, and on the whole equally astonishing situation of improvisation in which Westmalle and the Order abandoned these heroic monks for a quarter of a century. That is not what we propose to undertake here. Our intention is simply to bring out once again several aspects of Dom Le Bail's physiognomy, as they appeared in this delicate mission, and at the same time to listen to the pulse of his community deprived of his presence for a whole year. We can really speak of a "sacrifice" accepted with generosity by Dom Anselme and his sons, who were in no way responsible for this unfortunate story.

In a letter dating from March, 1921, addressed to the Abbot General, Dom Norbert wrote from Rome:

> Most Reverend Father, the Reverend Father Abbot of Chimay has written to me that the Reverend Father Abbot of Westmalle has asked him to replace him in making the canonical visit in Congo. He refused, as you know, and has submitted to you the reasons which he feels do not permit him to accept to do so. He has asked me to intercede for him to Your Paternity with this same intention. Dom Anselme certainly has very serious reasons for remaining at the head of his community.
>
> On the other hand, the Visitation in Congo is absolutely necessary. The Holy See is going to demand it, if we postpone making it. It is certainly annoying that the Abbot of Westmalle, Dom Hermann, is not going himself to visit his daughter-house. He must have explained to you his reasons for not going. And if he really cannot go to Congo, one can understand that your Paternity cannot consider sending an old man or someone who is sick. Among the young abbots who are in good form, Dom Anselme seems to me, in fact, to be the one most indicated for this fatiguing and especially delicate mission. So I am going to write to him to urge him to accept by devotedness to our Order.

He did not delay in writing this letter. That same month of March, Dom Norbert wrote to Dom Anselme:

> My dear Reverend Father, I really feel sorry for you! But I do not see how it is possible to get you out of this terrible job: make your sacrifice. After all, the community can get along without you for several months, with Fr. Charles or Fr. Godefroid at the helm . . . You were right to refuse first and to give your reasons for doing so. But I do not see how you can obstinately continue to refuse. There has to be a visitor. Who? Thanks for offering.

At the end of his letter Dom Norbert wrote: "I hope we will see one another before your excursion in Africa." Speaking of an "excursion" was no doubt meant to be humorous, but in any case it was bitter humor. We will have the occasion to see that. As soon as Dom Anselme accepted, tongues started wagging. On March

13 Dom Anselme received a letter from the Abbot General Dom Augustine, written at Cîteaux:

> My dear Reverend Father, I have just received your nice letter and I begin by telling you that I understand that you dread the weighty task which the Abbot of Westmalle has asked you to assume. It is completely natural that you are concerned about your community that you are going to leave for five or six months. But you have heard directly from Dom Hermann what the situation is down there. He must also have told you that his health makes it impossible for him to undertake such a long trip. On the other hand, the religious in Congo have expressed their desire that the Visitation should be made by either Dom Norbert or you. As it is, with important affairs pending, it is totally impossible for Dom Norbert to leave Rome this year. As for you, you have a community that is going along well; you have responsible assistants, to the point that you were able to be away during the war without anything notably prejudicial happening on either the spiritual or temporal level, which would have given you a reason to lament. By accepting this mission you are rendering an important service, first of all to the house in Congo, then after that to Dom Hermann, and finally to the whole Order. I thank you, in advance, very sincerely. You understand very well that it is not only a question of going down there simply to find out what the situation is. You must —as soon as possible—find solutions for urgent matters which can be rectified while you are there; for other matters, you should bring back all the information possible. Without speaking about the fatigue the voyage will cause, you must foresee that you will find real and important difficulties down there. Perhaps they will be less than we fear and, after a period of agitation at first, you will find yourself in presence of men of good will who are inclined to submit. You will need good health to accomplish the mission you have accepted. We ask Our Lady of Cîteaux to grant you her help and protection, to bless your work, and to incline hearts to submission. You know that King Leopold did not ask us to found a mission, but to create a monastery of Trappists. Instead of that, our religious have established a mission, and consequently we have deviated: at present we have a work to which we have not been

> called, and for which we are not made. There is also rebellion against Fr. G. which has to be calmed down . . . Good health and good courage, my dear Reverend Father.

This sounds like someone sending a candidate for martyrdom into an arena full of wild beasts. Actually, two enormous problems, though not of the same type, were waiting for the Visitor.

The first and most important problem was the situation which both Westmalle and the Order had permitted to exist during the last twenty-five years: Trappist Fathers of the Strict Observance, sent to found a monastery according to the Usages and Customs of Cîteaux, had rapidly become missionary religious. By the force of circumstances, of course. This case is not the only one: during the same period the Benedictines of the Abbey Saint-André de Bruges, like the Trappists of Westmalle, had generously accepted a romantic but poorly-informed invitation from King Leopold II. The idea was that European monks could accomplish in Africa what the great medieval monasteries had accomplished as centers of spirituality, culture and economy, and that the surrounding native populations would come to settle near the monastery and establish a "Christian civilization." This, however, meant forgetting the fact that the medieval monks had been preceded in Europe by evangelizing and missionary monks during several centuries. The Benedictines quickly understood, accepted and encouraged this inescapable missionary aspect of monastic implantation in Congo. Once the Trappists were settled there, they realized, understood and respected this same missionary urgency. But the Trappist Strict Observance, heir of recent centuries, no longer remembered the Cistercian Fathers who were preachers and travelers.

According to Saint Bernard's expressions, was the mission of the Trappists in Congo not "a canal which poured out its water at the same time it received it?" or was it "a vase that fills itself up first and shares only its superabundance?" This dilemma is not as simple as it may appear in writing. Where the monks actually were, it was completely different. In the archives a very detailed account has been preserved of the period when the Trappists were in Belgian Congo, from their first steps on African soil at Boma, on May 2, 1894 until the last statistics of their Cistercian missionary work: 1 principal house, 3 secondary posts, 12 Fathers, 8 Brothers, 14 Sisters, 168 catechists, 3,286 baptisms, 215,219 communions, 553 Christian marriages, 20,623 living Christians, 5,578 Christian families; 5725 catechumens, 2 orphanages providing for 108 orphans, 7 schools for 237 pupils, 2 pharmacies, 2 hospitals, and 4 shelters for widows. This breath-taking account which of itself would deserve a monograph, comes from the hand of Father Rumoldus Dries of Tegelen, in 1919. In his introduction, Father Rumoldus referred to the traditional missionary dimension of the Cistercian vocation:

> Faithful to their institution as a contemplative Order, during the more than eight centuries of their existence the Cistercians have nevertheless inherited the apostolic spirit which has always characterized the valiant Benedictine family of which they are one of the most flourishing branches. Saint Bernard already gave witness to this by sending colonies of monks to distant, barbarian regions in Pomerania, Lithuania, and on the Scandinavian coast. More recently, numerous hosts of Cistercian-Trappists transplanted in Bosnia, Syria, Palestine, on the coasts of China and Japan, in Oceania and on the beaches of southeast Africa give witness to this. If some of them have had as goal to propagate the monastic life, others have had to work among the native peoples to sow the seeds of Christianity. The foundation in Oceania was closed when one of the monks was killed by cannibals of New Pomerania. The foundation of Natal, today a distinct Congregation, enjoys good results in its work in both the colony on the Cape and in Rhodesia.

These precious pages by Father Rumoldus no doubt helped Dom Anselme quite a bit to look with respect and comprehension at the situation he was about to discover. We will come back to this after explaining the second problem that was awaiting the canonical Visitor.

This problem was a conflict between persons: Father G., the superior of the whole Trappist mission, and Father L. who, exasperated by the authoritarian ways of his superior, had ostensibly left the monastic life without any canonical procedure and had become—as was said at that time—an apostate. When Dom Anselme set foot on African soil, the apostate priest had a little commercial venture set up on the Upper-Tshuapa river, whereas Fr. G., the superior, who had returned from a visit to Westmalle, was temporarily living with the Apostolic Vicar in Léopoldville. What kept Fr. G. from taking up his duties again in the principal house in Bokuma, which was a one-day trip from Coquilhatville by steamboat? Fear, because Fr. L. had told everyone who was willing to listen to him that if the superior resumed his duties again he was going to reveal a series of moral and financial scandals that Fr. G. was guilty of, and that he would return to Bokuma to beat him up.

We are beginning to understand why the Father Abbot, who had left normally for six months, remained in Congo for a year, from March, 1921 until February, 1922. Conscious of his responsibilities, he was going to make the Visitation with tenacity and discretion, obliged as he was to take upon himself the burden of twenty-five years of improvisation and neglect on the part of the Order. The majority of the monks at Scourmont were ignorant of how complex the abbot's task was and attributed his extended stay in Africa to his taste for what is exotic, whereas he himself wrote to his aunt: "The Africa that I am traveling around is not as beautiful as Séglien. It is a continuous forest, cut through by rivers and marshes." To Scourmont, Dom Anselme wrote that he never let a day pass by without thinking of his dear sons, and of each one's face, one after another. He knew, furthermore, that their affection accompanied him. When he arrived at Leopoldville on May 14, a letter from Scourmont was waiting for him at the Apostolic Vicariate.

> Reverend Father, we are still under the impression of your last instructions, of your last words, your leave-taking in which you summarized so well the wish of Our Lord on the evening of his Paschal meal of love: "*Ut sit unum,*" and on the days following his Paschal triumph: "*Pax vobis.*" After your departure we listened for a long time to the echo of these words in the lessons of the Gospel and in the Mysteries of the season.

And it seemed to us that this year, for the monks of St-Joseph, there was beneath the divine words a prolongation of your voice, Reverend Father, which each time blended with Jesus' voice to ask us to be unceasingly what you have made of us, your sons, the sons of your soul and your thought, obedient sons, resolutely united in Peace in this dwelling place of divine love which is our community of Scourmont.

And the days have come and gone one after another until this 21st day of April, your patronal feast day! It is the happy occasion which permits your dear community to surround you with one heart and one love, to offer you a new token of its deep attachment. It is doing so, my Reverend Father, with this abandonment of holy intimacy and respectful affection which characterizes the privileged family where Jesus Christ truly rules. I do not know what inspiration gave me the idea last year to celebrate your feast day more than usual, to scatter a few flowers on your path that day, and to express in a rather solemn manner some simple words in order to crystallize, if I may say it this way, our sentiments as sons, sons more and more devoted to their Father. Was this something new? No! Everything was according to Tradition. It was, if one would want to put it this way, a charming parenthesis which summarized all the habitual personal wishes of each one and expressed them by one wish: something stronger, something like a public manifestation of the virtue of thanksgiving.

There was an evening that we set aside for this little surprise. Do you remember, Reverend Father? The reading at Compline that evening went with the circumstance; perhaps it was not very liturgical but how warm and full of life! We were all at our places. One single person was to be the last, and it had to be you, Reverend Father. Above our heads, the electric lights glowed in the Chapter room. At your place flowers and greenery were strewn about like a carpet. As you came in the monks applauded. Then there were greetings and music. And to conclude we listened to your great heart speaking, and telling us again with gentle emotion that you love us, just as we love you.

Who would have guessed, during those hours, that one year later our thoughts would go beyond this Continent, make their way across the ocean, and faithfully follow the wake of a ship

> sailing toward Africa? And all that to be with you, my Reverend Father, to find you again on the day we are waiting for, gathered together once more around you on this feast of Saint Anselme. Here we are; no one is missing. We are no doubt a little sad because of this forced separation, but we are resigned to it, confident that you will return soon, and more anxious than ever to express vocally our great respect, our filial attachment, our affection and our tenderness—in one word, everything that is most generous and affable—that our childlike hearts can feel and express for the one who is our Father. Our thoughts remain with you and do not leave you. Our prayer each day is united to and blends with your prayer to obtain from the Divine Master his protection on your long voyage, the success of the mission entrusted to you, and finally your return among us. This prayer will rise to heaven more fervently on this day, your feast day, and by our holy Sacrifices and Communions we will implore in a special way this grace: to preserve you in the deep affection of our hearts for many more long years, for the enlightened direction of our souls and for the ever-increasing prosperity of our dear Abbey.

This letter was written by Father Godefroid, his Prior, to whom Dom Anselme had entrusted the direction of the community. His signature was followed by 66 more signatures, those of the monks of Scourmont.

How fortunate is the Abbot who receives in return the tenderness he lavishes on his sons! In contrast, Dom Anselme had in his pocket a rather bitter letter for the courageous monks in Congo from Dom Augustine, Abbot General of Cîteaux, which echoed what Dom Hermann of Westmalle thought:

> Our very dear sons of Saint-Joseph in Congo, according to the order given to us by the Sacred Congregation of the Propaganda and in keeping with the desire expressed by your Very Reverend Father Immediate, we have delegated for the Regular Visitation of your house the Very Reverend Father Abbot of Chimay, Dom Anselme, who by his acceptance has shown very great dedication to the Order, to Westmalle, to Dom Hermann, and also to you, your community and your mission. We are

> persuaded that you realize how grateful you should be to him for this, and it is for this reason that we tell you with what sentiments you should receive the Reverend Father Visitor, as our delegate.
>
> You can imagine how strange and humiliating Dom Hermann found your desire that this Visitation should not be made by him. In the end, things are working out well because the state of his health would not have permitted him to make such a long and tiring trip.
>
> Permit me to add that in no way do we see how or for what reason the community of Westmalle and your Reverend Father Immediate could have lost the esteem of your community. On the contrary, we would consider it to be a real misfortune, and like a signal of decadence with regard to your work in the Congo, if "the enemy-man" would lessen in your hearts your attachment to your Mother house and your Father Immediate, and if the bonds which unite you to them would be loosened. Personnel, resources, affection, devoted help, advice, care given to those who come back for some rest, all that would be compromised. We do not want to say anything more about this. We have the greatest confidence in the Reverend Father Visitor's spirit of faith and prudence. And we pray to God to incline your souls to the most complete submission to the measures which he will judge opportune to take.

We could not find anything better illustrating the infantile ecclesiastical style, mixing suspicion with threats. But as we could expect, Dom Anselme did not enter into this game. His reputation as an open and cordial man had preceded his arrival. And he counted on making this Visitation without any preconceived ideas, except the a priori of sympathy and respect. When he arrived his first consolation was a letter he received from the notorious apostate Fr. L., not as terrible, it would seem, as what was imagined at Westmalle. "My very Reverend Dom Anselme, I have only one desire, and that is to see you as soon as possible. Be assured, Father: you will not have to deal with a lost son or a prodigal child. My only objective is that everything may be arranged for the best. And you can be persuaded that it is not from my side that you will run into difficulties. While awaiting the happiness of meeting you, I remain your humble servant."

So things were starting out well. The astonishing number of kilometers covered by Dom Anselme is the gauge of his concern for intellectual and monastic truth. By respect for his memory, we are going to take the trouble and time to relate here how he employed his time during his visit to Congo: This account is at the same time a page of the anthology of the history of Belgian missions, and a spiritual experience which marked Dom Le Bail's heart for the rest of his life. There is no doubt that he was "different" when he came back from this canonical Visitation.

> Having left Antwerp on Thursday, April 21, 1921, I arrived at Leopoldville on May 14. Since I had to wait for a week at Leopoldville for a boat to take me to Upper-Congo, I had time to speak with the Apostolic Vicar and Reverend Father G., superior of the mission, who has returned from Westmalle and has been living in this place since March. I left Kinshasa on May 22 and arrived at Coquilhatville the evening of Saturday, the 28th. All the Fathers of the Mission had already been convoked there. Seven of the ten could attend, whereas three Fathers were unable to come because of the needs of their posts of duty. Tuesday, May 31, however, all of them were present together, so I proceeded with opening the Regular Visitation.
>
> The first day, in a general session, the document concerning the delegation and powers of the Visitor was read, as well as the letters accompanying it. I presented the questions which we would treat of, drew them up—in French and Flemish—in the form of a program, and communicated them to each one. Conversations in group and meetings with the individual brothers followed on June 1 and 2; on Friday, June 3 , the feast of the Sacred Heart, this first session was closed by a new general session.
>
> During this opening session no decisions, no rulings were made. For the religious, it was a time for considering according to both law and perfection the question of a superior, the question of monastic life and that of the apostolic life, as well as the present state and future possibilities of the Mission. I strived to show them the different aspects of these questions; and I invited them to reflect, while telling them also that they would have several months before the Visitation would be closed. As for me, I was both establishing contact with the community

and getting used to African folkways. It would take me several months to familiarize myself with the special aspects of African life.

Delegated to visit the community and the Mission, I had to go around to all the posts, see the religious and how things were going in each place, and even, to complete my instruction—in my opinion—, travel around this territory of evangelization like a missionary.

Our Cistercians in Belgian Congo occupy at present the whole district of the Equator, formed by the basin of the Ruki river and its tributaries, that is to say, about 660 km. long and 200 to 250 km. wide.

On this territory of their apostolate our Fathers possess five posts where there is permanent residence, as follows: 1) Bokuma, on the Riki, one day by steamboat from Coquilhatville: the central post, with the following personnel when I arrived: 3 Fathers, 2 Brothers. 2) Coquilhatville, the main place in the province and the district, with a population of 250 whites, 4000 blacks: personnel: 2 Fathers, 4 brothers, one Father on leave in Europe. 3) Bamania, a trek of two hours from Coquilhatville, further inland: personnel: 2 Fathers, 1 Brother. 4) Bokoté, on the Tshuapa, a tributary of the Ruki, at 4 days by steamboat from Coquilhatville: personnel: 2 Fathers, 2 Brothers. 5) Wafania, on the Monboyo, a tributary of the Ruki, 6 days by steamboat from Coquilhatville: personnel: 3 Fathers, 1 Brother. Total: 14 Fathers —with the Reverend Father Superior—of whom 3 have not made stability; 10 Brothers, of whom four have not made stability; for a total of 24 persons.

As soon as the Visitation was opened I undertook visiting these posts and their territory. From June 4th until 7th at Bamania; from the 8th until the 13th at Coq. On June 13 I left for Wafania. That evening I went on to Bokuma and continued my voyage the next morning. Arriving at Wafania on Saturday, June 18, I stayed at this place until Monday, the 27th. On that date, the 27th, I set out in a caravan accompanied by two Fathers. During 21 days we traveled through a part of the territory dependent on Wafania and part of the territory dependent on Bokoté, visiting the groups of Christians and stopping at farm/chapels. Traveling in this caravan we covered about 250 kms, crossing diagonally the whole district of the Equator and the territory of the Mission. July 17 we arrived at Bokoté and stayed at this post until the 30th of the same month. A week was sufficient, but we had to wait until July 30 for the steamboat. That day I left for Upper-Tshuapa. Father L. has a little store set up beside this river. I wanted to see him—to take steps to meet him, as Canon Law asks superiors to do in such cases—and furthermore, to reply to everyone's desire, that of the apostate himself, and also the desire of my heart. Fr. Gregory Van Dun, the rector at Bokoté and Fr. George Dubrulle, rector of Wafania—two of the most senior Fathers of the Mission—accompanied me. We arrived at Wita, the end of our journey, the evening of August 3. Three days of conversation sufficed. We had to wait until August 14 for a boat. Fr. L. traveled with us as far as Bokoté. I traveled down to Bokuma in a pirogue, arriving Sunday, August 21. This five-day trip in a pirogue enabled me to visit the Christian communities of Tshuapa and Busira, situated on the shore: we stopped at different farm/chapels. From August 21 until the 27th I stayed at Bokuma. At each post I was able to talk to all the members of the community, Fathers and Brothers, those who did not have their stability there just as well as the others, and I listened to each one individually. I examined the accounts and the overall state of temporal administration. In addition, at each post and in the farm-chapels I observed—to the extent that it was possible and useful—the work of evangelization of the black people. It seemed to me to be profitable to try to penetrate the sentiments of the blacks themselves, to enter into contact with them, to speak to them as a group in their native language in order to be able to judge more accurately the work of the Monk-Missionaries. Thus this detailed inspection was completed at the end of August. The time had come to conclude. I could not do this without seeing the Rev. Fr. Superior and the Apostolic Vicar. Both were at Leopoldville. I left Bokuma on August 27, and arrived at Leopoldville September 3. The Apostolic Vicar is absent, and yet I need his advice for everything; I have to wait for his decisions concerning the apostate suspended by the Ordinary. While awaiting his return I go to Kisantu, the principal mission of the Jesuit Fathers in Lower Congo. There I can be sure of finding good advice and someone with experience in everything concerning the Mission in Belgian Congo. On my arrival there on

> September 5, I have time to converse at leisure with Rev. Fr. G., the Superior until the 13th. On September 13, Msgr. Van Ronslé arrives at Boma and stops at Kisantu. I explain my mission to him. The 14th he gives me a reply concerning Fr. L., who must return to Europe to be reinstated from his suspension. The 15th, he suggests to Rev. Fr. G. that he resign as Superior in order to facilitate the whole solution. Msgr. De Vos, Apostolic Prefect of Lower Congo, gives the same advice. I am waiting. I consult them myself. The 16th, I accept the resignation of the Father Superior. The 17th, I go back to Leopoldville. Since there was no boat, I have to wait until September 28 to go back up the Congo as far as Coquilhatville. I arrive there on Wednesday, October 5. So the trip took 40 days: from August 27 until October 5. October 6, since the Governor General of Congo was passing through Coquilhatville, I feel I should go and pay my respects to him, and offer him those of the Trappist Fathers' Mission.

Let us interrupt this account for a moment to point out that the Scourmont monks, counting the days and months, were beginning to stamp their feet impatiently. A flood of letters went out to the Father Abbot. The first was dated October 24, 1921:

> Eight years have gone by since your abbatial blessing; eight years that Chimay has been living under your blessed crozier. Alas, what a trial it is for us to look back over these eight years: nearly five years of absence! But we do not know our Father! Scarcely had he been given back to us when he was taken away from us again! Frankly, it is not very gay for us. We have plenty of reasons to say that life is a series of separations, a series of departures and ruptures. Here, at Chimay, in your Reverence's worthy Abbey, we are all stamping our feet with impatience and lonesomeness. We are waiting for you, we wait for news of you, and the boats do not arrive. What in the world are you doing? Have they elected you Abbot of Congo? If that is the case, a lot of us are going to take off right away, to go and give you a hand. When is a letter from you going to arrive telling us you are leaving, or, better still, a telegram notifying us of the day of your arrival? Don't put it off, Father! Here we are preparing for your return: there is like a renewal of life which is taking hold of all of us because we want to show you that Chimay is worthy of your care and solicitude.

Dom Anselme, however, was far from having terminated:

> I cannot yet fix the date for the Fathers to have their general meeting. The new Apostolic Vicar of the Mission, Msgr. de Boeck, will be arriving from Europe to assume direction of the Apostolic Vicariate of New-Antwerp, on which the Trappists will depend from now on. I must see him for some shop talk and about the powers of the Superior and head of the Mission. He is to arrive at Coquilhatville on October 12. All the Fathers who have made their stability here have been convoked, and consequently everyone will be assembled at Bokuma on October 28. The retreat will begin that very day. It will be preached in Flemish—to suit everyone best—by a Jesuit from Lower Congo. It will last five days; I myself will close the retreat the morning of November 2.

That same day, November 2, another letter arrived from Scourmont, as impatient as it was naive:

> Have you received the two chasubles in good condition? Do you need anything for your return trip? Isn't it so, Father Abbot, that you will soon be coming back, in two or three weeks? Here, we are lonesome for you. It is so empty.

Well, no, the Father Abbot would not be coming back so soon:

> This second day we began our meetings to close the Regular Visitation. They lasted from November 2 until November 11, and took thirty-two hours of active sessions. These meetings had as goal to explain the decisions of the Regular Visitation. The abundance of material and the necessity of explaining each thing in a very clear way made this meeting take such a long time. I went back over the program which I had drawn up after my arrival and then developed it: the charge of the superior, monastic questions, apostolic questions. I made a decision or gave a directive on each thing; I spoke in French and, when it was necessary, had what I said translated into Flemish; I explained my remarks, listened to the observations made publicly or privately by the religious, and drew up a definitive text. During these long sessions all the religious showed great fidelity and attention to all the questions. Their cordiality and

> unanimity were continual, and that gave everyone the joy of community life for a few days. By this way of closing the Visitation I wanted, furthermore, to set a precedent for annual meetings of the whole Community of Congo, assembling everyone together at least once a year to reflect during a retreat, to renew the bonds of fraternity and to treat of family matters all together. On November 11 each one could return to his post. As for me, I used the last days of November to draw up the final Visitation Card and settle questions which concerned the superior more specially. I added two short trips—part of the Visitation—to two Christian settlements near Bokuma. I got ready to take the boat for Europe in the middle of December, when a last attempt and last compliance made me hope to have P. L. return with me, as I am going to explain. Seeing that my waiting would go on indefinitely, I decided to leave alone. My mission in Belgian Congo was finished.

Before Dom Anselme set out for Europe, he was addressed by the chief of the Bolima catechists, Boniface Bakutu, in an ardent supplication which must have touched his heart profoundly: We reproduce it here with a minimum of stylistic corrections: It expresses very well the confidence the Father Abbot had shown toward the populations of black people and their monk-missionaries:

> To the very Reverend Father Visitor, all of us, Christian children and catechists of Ikelemba, we come to you very respectfully to put before you our pitiful desire. We have here 6,000 Christians, and also pagans, and we have no Fathers in our country. Why? From the year 1913, when the Fathers left Bombimba and Ifutu to go to Bokoté, there were only 1400 Christians. I remained all alone with the catechists of Ikelemba, to give them lessons. Then, three times a year Brother Pancratius came to visit the Christians everywhere in the whole region and to administer the sacraments. Today there are 6,000 Christians. Why don't we have any Fathers? All of us, your black Christian children of Ikelemba, ask you to help us, by mercy and charity, in our need to have priests to establish a mission at Bolima. Many of our Christian friends have died without receiving the

last Sacraments, because there were no priests. We thirst to see you again among us at Bolima. Our Lord Jesus Christ became man because he wanted to save the world. You, our Father Visitor, have mercy on us, and give us Fathers to establish a mission. You came to visit the place where your Christian children live. I and the Christians of Ikelemba, we sent you 13 chickens and 44 eggs. But because you had left Coquilhatville, what we sent is in the hands of Fr. Robert. All these words, we say them with faith, hope and charity. I dare to hope, Very Reverend Father Visitor, that you will look well into our situation and give us satisfaction, if possible.

How could European problems of Usages and Customs of the Strict Observance take precedence over these cries of distress coming from a young Church? And yet, that is what would happen. . . .

After leaving Coquilhatville on January 4, I went directly down to Boma, but not without saying goodbye to Msgr. Van Ronslé at Leopoldville. He has always been so good and helpful to our Fathers, and has been a precious helper and advisor to me during my whole mission. At Boma, I wanted to see the Governor General. To my great regret, he was absent. A relationship with the government is necessary and extremely important in the Colonies. I left from Boma on the Anversville on January 28, 1922, and arrived at Antwerp on February 2, 1922.

Scarcely had he informed his monks of the date of his return when he received a letter from his faithful secretary which—one can well imagine—reflected the sentiments of all the Scourmont monks:

I want to be one of the first to come to wish you welcome to our European soil, on your return after this absence eleven-months long! I would like to be on the dock at Antwerp to greet you. You are coming back to us. Father! What joy for all of us! I have a strong feeling that this return must be a cause of joy for you too, but also one of some intense melancholy. You are going to assume a weighty task, so heavy for your shoulders

> and your paternal heart . . . I prepared your quarters at the Abbey with all my heart. I want to be there to give you back your keys . . . I dreamed of sending you a lovely bouquet of fragrant flowers from our gardens, which would be waiting for you on the table at Westmalle.

Actually, Dom Anselme was going to put on the table at Westmalle a package of papers—analyses and conclusions of his canonical Visitation – which were going to please neither the Father Immediate nor Father G. (the former superior of the Mission, who had resigned), who had no intention of accepting them. What they wanted was to suppress the mission posts, make a Trappist foundation, bring the monk-missionaries back into the enclosure and send any objectors back to Westmalle. As for Dom Le Bail, he came to conclusions which were totally different:

> The work of the Trappist Fathers in Congo is a mission and not a monastery. Their zeal, their devoted work, their good conduct, have been rewarded by the formation—in twenty-five years—of a Christian population of 23,000 faithful, 10,000 living catechumens and an intense Christian life.
>
> In my opinion, this work cannot be other than missionary.
>
> The present personnel cannot reasonably be obliged to live the Cistercian monastic life in Congo in one single regular house. To support this statement, we give the following reasons: Firstly, since 1895, and especially since 1900, their work has been a Mission. Secondly, the priests—and even some of the lay brothers—who are presently in this community entered a monastery in Europe with the intention of going to Congo as missionaries. The bulletins of the work "*Missiewerk*", from 1904 until 1913, give witness to that. Other monks, who entered regular monasteries in Europe without this intention, have been in Congo for many years: they went there to be missionaries, and they are in fact missionaries. Thirdly: at present 11 of the 13 priests have expressed their desire to remain missionaries, as they are now. To sum up, in our opinion, to put all these people together in the same place under the Rule of Cîteaux would be to demolish a legitimately acquired situation. It would be difficult for the majority and even detrimental for

> several of the monks, because of the dangers for Europeans living in enclosure in Congo.
>
> As a result of our own experience, we affirm that the Order of Cîteaux has no advantage, and can not yet desire at present, to found a regular community following the Cistercian statutes of the Strict Observance in this country of the Equator in the Belgian Congo. We do not believe that Europeans can follow the regular observances of the Order near the Equator. Not only would it be dangerous for the monks' health for them to be held to Cistercian rules, but what is more, we believe that in this region it is not good for the soul to observe enclosure and to devote oneself assiduously to the solemn celebration of the Divine Office and spiritual reading, to the exclusion of apostolic works. And yet, these observances are essential to the monastic contemplative life. On the other hand, we cannot hope for native recruitment of penitent and contemplative monks before 50 years or perhaps more. Consequently the communities would have to obtain their recruitment from Europe.
>
> Our opinion, therefore, is that it is advantageous for the Order of Cistercians, and also for the Cistercian community in Belgian Congo, to be established and organized as an apostolic work.

The General Chapter decided otherwise and obstinately wanted to adhere to its opinion. Fortunately Rome took the matter up and, by according them exclaustration, encouraged the Trappists in Congo to remain missionaries. Dom Anselme never expressed the slightest bitterness. He felt that he had fulfilled his task with discernment. And with his heart. He regularly sent books, magazines and dictionaries to his dear missionary brothers, who repaid him with grateful and affectionate letters.

20

When two abbots become close friends

Up until the time of his return from Congo we have strictly followed the chronology of Dom Anselme's life, because each year brought something new in his existence. From now on we will have to span several years at a time, as we treat of certain themes and characteristics of his abbacy. Nevertheless, we will try to date them when it will be possible or useful to do so. As we do this, we will bring out new traits of the character of this astonishing man who, we hope, has already become closer to us.

One of the first sources from which we will draw is the assiduous correspondence—continuous from 1914 until 1935—between Dom Anselme Le Bail, Abbot of Scourmont, and Dom Alexis Presse, Abbot of Tamié. No intimate personal notes of Dom Anselme are extant from this period, even though he wrote some. But, in his letters to Father Alexis, confidential remarks—sometimes biting ones—and bits of humor, always liberating—raise a corner of the veil which covered Dom Anselme's heart in the solitude that is the lot of all those who bear such responsibilities.

Astonishing was the meeting, and still more astonishing the friendship which was born and deepened between these two men who had very different ideas and were to have such very different itineraries. At the beginning, however, there were several common points which made them congenial to one another. First of all, they were both Bretons—which is certainly something. Without having known each other when they were young, they were born in places only a few dozen kilometers apart, Emmanuel Le Bail five years before Mathurin Presse. They both began their schooling with the Lammenais Brothers. They both attended the

Pardon of Sainte Anne d'Auray. And when Emmanuel Le Bail made his decisive retreat at Timadeuc in 1904, Mathurin Presse had already been a novice there for a year, with the name of Br. Alexis. At that time, however, there was no contact between the two of them.

It seems that they first noticed their fellow-feeling at the General Chapter of 1913, which Dom Anselme attended as Abbot, and Father Alexis as a student in Rome who had been asked to propose a reform of the Cistercian liturgy. Did each of them have a presentiment that he wanted a return to what was "authentic" (the word which quickly became Father Alexis' key-word)? The first letter, which began their long and faithful correspondence, was from Dom Alexis in 1914. We have only Dom Anselme's reply. What could have been in Father Alexis' letter? No doubt the first intuitions of a dream that he would describe several years later, when describing an imaginary monastery, "La Paix Notre Dame," where life would go along in authentic observance of the Rule of Saint Benedict, a kind of resurrection of a Cistercian monastery of the first era. Daniel-Rops described it this way: "Everything the first sons of Saint Bernard had thought of and admitted as being true practices should be taken as a rule for the way of living. It was like a kind of historical re-construction which had the advantage of making it possible to by-pass certain customs—one might say excesses—but it was not at all sure that it could be inserted into the context of life in the twentieth century."

Here is Father Alexis' imaginary monastery:

> I see Rancé, a man in full maturity, a great Lord more or less rakish, a prelate and ecclesiastic not very edifying, to say the least. In the midst of all the vain things in the world, I see him touched by grace and transformed. With his ardent spirit and very passionate nature, he no longer dreams of anything but one single thing: being saved. Now, for that, he will have to expiate the past and assure the future; expiate a very guilty past which frightens him because of his iniquities and requires severe penance. His salvation can be at this price alone. It was with these sentiments that the convert entered the Order. It

> would be with these sentiments that he would make his novitiate. It was in this spirit that he interpreted the Rule of Saint Benedict. His reform would be a reform of penance, but it would be neither that of primitive Cîteaux nor that of the Benedictine school of Christ.
>
> Personally, I want to be authentic, and therefore, Cistercian. I bear that name, and I have made profession of it. So logically I should go back to the tradition of our Fathers. It seemed to me, as it had seemed to them, that the God-Truth requires us to return to what is true, to what is authentic, in spite of and contrary to everything and everybody. We do not want to be of the common, nor of the strict, nor of the middle observance of Cîteaux. We want to be and try to be simply and purely Cistercians.

To these remarks, which were already fiery, Dom Anselme replied serenely and objectively:

> Thank you very much for communicating to me your notes and observations on the ideal Cistercian: I agree with you unhesitatingly and have never thought differently than you do, in spite of my being a headstrong Breton. I noticed with pleasure that for you the vital principle of the Cistercian Order is zeal for the integrity of the Rule. "*Regula ad litteram.*" It is a vital principle, I say, because where it is followed there is life; and where there are deviations, life has diminished or died out. Didn't our Fathers extend this principle to mean everything which was to contribute to their rule of life? Is it not for the same reason that they sought the integral purity of Gregorian chant, and the purity of the Vulgate Bible? I recently made this comparison in community, showing that in these preoccupations of our Fathers there was the same spirit: zeal for Tradition by a spirit of obedience, and keeping to what has been established by the Church as a norm for the life of monks. All this seems to me to have been confirmed by the primitive statutes which called for uniformity among the Houses of our Order.

This first exchange of letters shows from the outset the difference in the sensibility of Dom Anselme and of Father Alexis: the latter would always be listened to with respect, but never encouraged in his excesses. Less concerned with setting up an authentic exterior framework, Dom Anselme aimed at interior renewal of the spiritual reality. "Come," he wrote to Father Alexis, "it would do both of us good to meet. Here, at Scourmont, we are working with Father Berlière on a return to the treatises of our Fathers."

Basically, what would always separate the two monk "reformers" was that Dom Alexis would never be able to refrain from accompanying his concrete reforms with intellectual arguments that were harsh and which both provoked and produced inevitable conflicts and excommunications, whereas Dom Anselme would be pragmatic, audacious surely, but able to deflate criticism by his sense of humor. On a more profound level perhaps, Dom Alexis' superiors always noticed a kind of stubbornness in him which they said came close to pride, or in any case strong self-will; whereas Dom Anselme's superiors were unanimous in recognizing in him flawless obedience. This did not prevent Dom Anselme from sometimes launching a few oxygen balloons in the Cistercian heavens. For example, he announced at a General Chapter that he had begun having sinks with running water installed in the monks' alcoves. When he saw the scandalized reaction of his peers, he quite simply sent a telegram to Scourmont: "Stop work on the dormitory." Likewise, he had dispensed from the Offices of Sext and None his young scholastics who had classes. He announced in Chapter: "Our young student brothers are workmen "in spirituality." Reprimanded by the Order, he immediately put a stop to this initiative. In the same way, he had allowed his dear sons to be able to have a cup of coffee and a little bread in the morning. After the visit of the Abbot of Timadeuc, who preached strict fasting, Dom Anselme re-established this practice without any bitterness. He wrote to his aunt:

> Strict fasting has been re-established and things are going just as well. I was very pleased with this new re-adoption of the strict Rule. One feels more like a monk. Don't they say that the Trappist monk sings powerfully, works powerfully, and fasts powerfully? So we are men "three times powerful." But what great frailty there is behind all that!

The Father Abbot Anselme was not surprised by his monks' frailty. Does Saint Benedict not recommend to his monks, in chapter 72 of his Rule, to "support with the greatest patience one another's weaknesses, whether they be of body or spirit"?

And concerning the abbot of the monastery, does Saint Benedict not say in chapters 2 and 64:

> If he has faithfully shepherded a restive and disobedient flock, striving always to cure their unhealthy ways, the shepherd will be acquitted at the Lord's judgment.
>
> In his teaching the Abbot must vary with circumstances, threatening and coaxing by turns, stern as a taskmaster, devoted and tender as only a father can be. With the undisciplined and restless, he will use firm argument; with the obedient, docile and patient, he will appeal for greater virtue, but as for the negligent and disdainful, we charge him to use reproof and rebuke. He should not gloss over the sins of those who err . . . but those who are evil or stubborn, arrogant or disobedient, he can curb only by blows or some other physical punishment. . . . He must know what a difficult and demanding burden he has undertaken: directing souls and serving a great variety of characters. One needs to be led on by tenderness, another by sternness and another by persuasion. Once in office, the abbot must keep constantly in mind the nature of the burden he has received, and remember to whom he will have to *give an account of his stewardship* (Lk 16:2). Let him recognize that his goal must be profit for the monks, not pre-eminence for himself. He should always *let mercy triumph over judgment* (Jas 2:13). He must hate vices, but love the brothers.[1]

So Father Abbot Le Bail was not surprised that he had before him a turbulent and intractable flock: monks wounded by spiritual maladies; brothers who were negligent, rebellious or sluggish; men who were mean and hardheaded. And he knew that he ought to let them experience his pastoral solicitude, obligingness, fondness, gentleness, patience, persuasion and mercy.

[1] Cf. *RB 1980*, Liturgical Press: Collegeville, MN, 1980. Editor, Timothy Fry, OSB, ch. 2 & 64, pp. 175–177 and 281–283.

On the other hand, what disconcerted him was that the monks did not show the same mercy among themselves that God and their Abbot showed them. At Scourmont, like everywhere else, the monks seemed to be relentless toward their brothers. Unfortunately, whereas neither the Rule of Saint Benedict nor the Benedictines recognize the notorious "Proclamations" in Chapter where brothers publicly denounce the disciplinary deviations of their brothers, the Trappists practiced this kind of "social control." It was a dangerous game. Dom Anselme confided to Dom Alexis:

> Individually, the ninety members of my community think they are "perfect." Each one judges himself in a very advantageous way, but is not stingy about disdaining or even scorning his brothers. So there are "90 I's" who are perfect, and still, our community life is not perfect. The reason for this is that the eighth commandment is not observed among us. We always judge our brothers in a negative way, rashly and without charity. Now, to judge something in a healthy way we must know the exact facts and appraise them according to right reason: two attitudes which are rare among monks.
>
> So, on the basis of simple appearances or vulgar stories, each one judges hastily and thinks he is endowed with infused knowledge. But is the one who judges not himself judged automatically, according to what Jesus said? So one must have great prudence in order to judge well, a kind of prudence which requires the virtues of consideration, knowledge, counsel and circumspection, enumerated by Saint Thomas. Too often we lack these.
>
> In your opinion, what would remedy this evil? Would it not be the habit of putting off one's first judgment until there is more adequate information? Is there not in this world a way to make people wise and discreet? A fortiori, shouldn't that be the way for monks. Please: let's be good! Let's be condescending toward our neighbor, conscious as we are of our own weakness and wretchedness. Judging others harshly is a sign of immaturity. The older one gets, the more one knows and accepts his deficiencies, which are deep and constant. What is the use of our abstinence, if a monk is carnivorous in spirit? Let us stop devouring each other. Let us be merciful.

The war years—1914–1918—made frequent correspondence impossible between Dom Anselme and Father Alexis. The latter advanced in his combat for return to authenticity. His declarations and articles became more and more alarming to his Superiors at Timadeuc and those of the Order. Paradoxically—but no doubt in an attempt to get him back in line—he was sent to Rome as Director of the house of higher studies for the Cistercian Order. To do so was to have poor knowledge of Father Alexis, who ravenously devoured numerous works on the origin of the Order and made friends with quite a few prelates who were close to Pope Pius X. He was called back to Timadeuc, preceded by a reputation of criticizing his Superiors in public and having talked about "the old practices and stupid (*encroutées*) traditions." Father Alexis denied this, but the damage was done. His presence became more and more unbearable for some of the older monks in the monastery. He wrote about his trials to Dom Anselme, who replied to him:

> Oh! What a great need for joy our poor humanity has, to be able to put up with this world! Is it perhaps simply a sign of its weakness? Life is a combat; and the combat means suffering, and often defeat. And defeat begets sadness. It would be enough to say to oneself, once and for all: life is joy for people who change and develop. So this combat is life; and life begets joy!

Shortly after, Father Alexis was sent away from Timadeuc and relegated to the Abbey of Bonnecombe, in Aveyron, to teach theology. However, after the death of Dom Brieuc Boutmy, the Abbot of Timadeuc, he was called back to his abbey to participate in the election of the new abbot. Scarcely had he arrived, when he realized that the "local gossips" were saying that he would probably be elected. However, Fr. Dominic Nogues was the one who was elected, on the first ballot and unanimously, consequently with Father Alexis' vote. Certain monks in the monastery were laughing up their sleeves or even sneering openly, like Father X who at the hour of manual work looked at Father Alexis with a sly smile and suggested: "We will offer our work for the monk who has just been elected, and also for those who were disappointed." The new abbot, a friend of Father Alexis, realized that the situation had become unbearable. Father Alexis was chosen to restore the Trappist monastery of Tamié. In his very beautiful book, *Boquen*, so respectful of Dom Alexis, Xavier Henry de Villeneuve described the state of Tamié when Father Alexis arrived:

> Perched at an altitude of approximately 900 meters, in a mountain pass much traveled in the past, the abbey of Tamié is situated in the massif of Bauges between Mount Sambuy and Mount Belle Étoile. Albertville, on the road which goes through the high mountains of Savoy, is only twelve kilometres away. The exposed location is not good, the climate is harsh; there is an abundance of snow which remains for long months. When the whole valley is green and the sun shines early in the morning, there is a majestic beauty about the place.
>
> In 1923 the monastery is in a pitiful state. The last abbot, Dom Dupic, retired in 1921. The Trappists camp in the buildings as best they can. Weeds grow up around the workshops and the monastic buildings are crumbling, ruined by the bad weather. Water leaks into the dormitories. The monks work to support themselves by making cheese, and live miserably from the sale of their products. The lack of prosperity at Tamié is due neither to the climate nor to its situation at high altitude in a hidden-away place, but from lack of order and regularity.
>
> A report drawn up in 1920 determined that 300,000 francs should be invested in urgent repairs, in order to clean up the house and make it habitable. The revenue of the abbey was scarcely 70,000 francs, whereas at least 100,000 francs were needed to provide for the monks' daily living. In the monastery there was neither blacksmith nor mason, nor tailor, nor cowherd. The monks were living in the cheese house, a domain ruled over by an omnipotent "religious." Even Dom Chautard had recommended: "One must not interfere with the brother in charge of the cheese; he is the one who makes a living for the community." The farm is spread out over an area of 50 hectares but only 5 can be cultivated, 14 are covered with woods and undergrowth, and the rest is made up of open fields

> and brush. No important repairs have been made since 1861. The window-frames need to be looked after, as well as the worm-eaten floors, the timbers and the roof. Restore the enclosure, clean and whitewash the moldy inside walls, all these things are clearly necessary and urgent. Between 1920 and 1922 a monk wanted to undertake this work under the authority of Dom Dupic, the abbot at that time, who was then living in the guesthouse. As soon as the first changes were begun he met with storms of objections and discontent. Quickly disabused, he soon left.
>
> The spiritual and human situation is scarcely more brilliant. There are 15 choir monks, the majority of whom have transferred here from the Abbey of the Grâce-Dieu. Twelve of them are priests, but two are infirm and others are worn out with age. Among the fifteen lay brothers, only four are originally from Savoy, and the lack of homogeneity is felt heavily in community. Two servants and one family brother help out.

Scarcely had Father Alexis arrived, when he thought of his faithful friend, Dom Anselme. He wrote to invite him to preach the community's retreat, and as a token of his insistence sent him some of Tamié's cheese. Dom Anselme replied:

> The cheese was so good! Good, really good! Look! I have kept a piece in my mouth right up until this minute; that is what has prevented me up until now from thanking you. Our poor Scourmont, more and more grey under persistent rain, is certainly unattractive in comparison to glorious Tamié. I would like to preach the retreat in November, because later on it is very difficult to reach Tamié. I am, of course, not afraid of the sleigh—on the contrary; but I don't want to be marooned at Tamié, in spite of all its glory and saints.

In 1925, Father Alexis was elected Abbot of Tamié. Dom Anselme hastened to write to him:

> I wish you many graces and, particularly, the gifts of prudence, wisdom, and perhaps patience especially, or at least above all other good things. I congratulate you, because it is you that Tamié needs. I feel sorry for you, and you can guess why. For

> me, the great advantage of your election is assurance that we will meet again and, I hope, work together.

In his letter Dom Anselme included a passage from Saint Bernard's *Letter 732* concerning the burden of an abbot of a monastery:

> This burden is that of souls, and souls that are sick. Those who are well, in fact, do not need anyone to carry them and they are not a weight. All those among yours whom you find sad or lax, or those who have trouble living, know that it is for those that you are Father, that you are Abbot. It is especially when you console, encourage or correct that you accomplish your work, that you bear your burden; and by carrying it you heal, and by healing you carry. If there is one who is healthy to the point that he helps you more than you help him, you are not a Father for that one but his equal, you are not his abbot but his companion. How can you complain then that the common life with certain brothers is a weight upon you rather than a source of strength? It is precisely so that you may be the source of strength for all that you have been chosen from among all of them, as being more sound and stronger than the others, capable of strengthening them all by God's grace, without needing to be strengthened by anyone.

Among the abbots present at the benediction of the Abbot, there was some whispering, heard and repeated, which we could summarize as follows: "The prophets give Dom Alexis Presse little chance of success. His failure will no doubt be complete, and that will satisfy those who find him cumbersome and pretentious." Having no idea that such remarks were being made about him, and such arrogance being so foreign to him, the poor and humble Abbot of Tamié wrote to Dom Anselme:

> It is God's work that has been entrusted to me. It is his business. In the way I carry out this work I should do all that I can—the little that I can in keeping with my own human possibilities—to accomplish reasonably what depends on me. That is the limit of my action. God does not ask me for more, and when I have

> accomplished that, I should remain quiet, in peace. As to positive results, to success, that does not concern me at all, and does not depend on me. It is up to God to make his work succeed.

Sorely lacking capable men, Dom Alexis began to beg help from Scourmont. It was first of all a Prior that he asked Dom Anselme for, because his was not cooperative, to say the least. The Abbot of Scourmont refused because he perspicaciously thought that a Prior coming from Chimay would be thought of as being Abbot Alexis' man. On this occasion, he sketched a profile of a Prior in the most sagacious Benedictine tradition:

> If I were to give you a Prior I would believe that I was doing a bad thing, both for the subject and for your community. Give you a Novice Master or a teacher: all right, I do not find any difficulty with that. Such sharing from outside is exterior to government, and does not touch the sensitive nerve of the community. But send you a Prior! The Prior is the mediator between the Abbot and the community. Now, you know that a mediator ought to participate in the nature of the two terms he ought to unite. In a monastery, he should be the man of both the Abbot and the community. A Prior whom I would send you would never be the man of the community. So it would be better if you would find a more or less good Prior among your own monks, but one of your own community rather than an excellent Prior from somewhere else. In any case that is my opinion, and I do not want to expose one of my brothers to the troubles of such a situation. Besides, at Scourmont, valuable men are not as numerous as one would believe. Most of them do not want to have any responsibilities, but simply to live the common life. So to ask one of my monks to be Prior at Tamié: imagine that! I sign: Father Abbot of Scourmont "*sine visceribus paternitatis*"—without paternal feelings—.
>
> As concerns your present Prior, one might suppose that he is more immature than treacherous. Think that he is perhaps someone who consoles the brothers who suffer because of you. Personally, I admit that my way of doing things is not perfect. And the monks do not lose their capacity of personal judgment

> when they make Profession. They are still free to evaluate, to judge or to criticize their Abbot's way of governing. They don't have to stir up a revolt against their Abbot. But they have the right to be reasonable persons, even if that implies risks. Leave to your Prior the care of making this discernment.

Little by little, however, Dom Alexis came to realize that opposition did not come only from his Prior; it was the majority of the monks who were secretly at odds with him. During a canonical visitation at Tamié the Father Immediate listened attentively to the opposition, floundering in the vagueness of its contradictions. The monks of Tamié, in fact, recognized on the one hand that their Abbot strove intensely to live a religious life, that he insisted on effective love of God, on generosity in the Lord's service and on the virtues of renouncement and poverty. But, on the other hand, they accused their Abbot of not understanding the importance of affective love, that is to say, especially his lack of interest in mental prayer, the way of the cross and, in a more general way, for devotions. The Abbot visitor concluded a bit too quickly: "At Tamié, there is no interior life."

When Dom Alexis read this report, he collapsed. He was persuaded that he had the whole community behind him, except for a few old monks whom he did not think he had to worry about. Had his two faithful friends, the Abbot of Saint Marie du Désert and the Abbot of Scourmont, not come to recognize his accomplishments and draw up a favorable evaluation of them? Dom Alexis, a man of truth, transmitted the results of the canonical visit to the community. On the benches of the Chapter room his monks were very upset; they protested, claiming their faithfulness to their Abbot. He expressed his bitterness in writing to Dom Anselme, who replied:

> I hadn't realized, from your Christmas letter, that you had so much trouble. All I think is that one should never despair of his community. Faced with divergence of ideas among his sons and even among his coadjutors, he should continue to have a certain confidence in them and, at all times, deference. An Abbot should govern amidst contradictions. You have done that with

> your Prior; you will continue to do it with your Sub-Prior and others. You ask me to accept at Scourmont Fr. X, who is particularly recalcitrant: I am willing to do so. My Prior and I will try to be discreet, that is, in this circumstance to respect your authority as Abbot of Tamié. However, when we are faced with a heart that is bitter we will not harshly stress this note of complete dependence. We will let him give voice to his complaints, but without encouraging him do so. We will try to make him understand. As you may guess, sometimes we will let what he says simply go by, as though we seem to approve of it. But you know that nothing can destroy our esteem and affection for you.

Since we are not writing a biography of Dom Alexis Presse here, but one of Dom Anselme Le Bail, we are not going to go too far and let ourselves get lost in the maze of the misadventures of the Abbot of Tamié, which finally led him to decide to leave Tamié to restore the Abbey of Boquen. But we will remain for a few minutes more in the company of these two friends by their correspondence, in order particularly to string a few of Dom Anselme's pearls:

First of all, concerning moderation, which the Abbot of Scourmont opposed to the Abbot of Tamié's lack of flexibility:

> In your place, I would compromise. Courage, then, and a bit of diplomacy in your way of governing. You complain about Father X., but his weak spot is a bit like your own: easily formed judgments expressed rudely, and being scandalized if someone is so weak as not to call the law the law.
>
> In my opinion, I would cut your caustic style out of your articles and statements. It poisons them and does not convince anyone. I did not like what you wrote about Rancé; I really didn't like it at all. And yet, you know that I am not a Rancé man. But when I hear someone speak of him with such raillery, my esteem for this man then comes back to life.
>
> Concerning our predecessors, you can say that some of them did not succeed very well in their projects. But do not ridicule them as though they had been blind or deaf. By doing so your proposals, which are often excellent, reap nothing but opposi-

> tion from most people. For example, your theoretical criticism of devotions should grant some latitude in practice: you cannot get everyone to renounce a little devotion which is tucked in a corner of the heart. You have to bargain, to give in about one devotion in order to win suppression of four other devotions. With devotions, you have to coax. Be suave, the way that your adoptive compatriot, Saint Francis de Sales, was.
>
> Soften up the way you talk. Calm your fierce eyes and your harsh Breton hands. If you want the end, choose the means. Be diplomatic, go ahead softly, as though you are indifferent to what the result may be.

Trial for trial: while Dom Alexis was being criticized for being intransigent about observances and the archaeological character of his desire to restore things, Dom Anselme was looked upon suspiciously because of the humaneness he was breathing into the observances and the resolutely modern character of his concern about renewal. Confidence for confidence:

> The great lords of the Order don't approve of our freedom here at Chimay to learn everything and say everything. They even condemn it. All right! We are lax. So let them pray for our conversion.
>
> Personally, I forget this shabby meanness by smoking a good cigar at night under the stars, or in the archives room, while thinking that there are people who pray that I will become a good monk again.

At the end of one General Chapter, the Father Abbot of a Trappist monastery in France unctuously offered everyone a glass of a newly macerated liqueur from his Abbey. Dom Le Bail lit a cigar instead, to astonishment as general as the Chapter of the same name. It is true that, in a domain as harmless as that of the Usages and Customs, Father Abbot Anselme took pleasure in upsetting the world of these Fathers of the Strict Observance. He knew very well what he was doing, and confided to Dom Alexis:

> With my Breton head, I refused to permit one of my monks to go to preach the retreat at Orval: it would be wrong, when one

> has the plague, to go and contaminate others. We will go to England, to Caldey, on an island, with its rats and rabbits, rabbits which they say are consumptive. That's just what we need.

We are going to put aside this correspondence with the following phrase written to Dom Alexis, which reveals very well Dom Anselme's openness of mind and heart: "Our differences are not an obstacle to friendship. There are enough points of likeness and agreement, and a little bit of discussion on our differences, which moreover are not harmful to keeping up our friendship."

It is touching, as the years passed, to follow the evolution of the titles Dom Le Bail used to address Dom Presse. They are tinted with tender humor:

> Very high Father, *altissime* doctor—Most Reverend Father—My most Reverend—My Reverend Father and friend—My Father and reverend friend—Very dear Father friend—Dear friend—Very dear friend—My friend—Friend.

21

Tireless hands and head

Dom Anselme was a great builder in face of the Eternal. Today, almost nothing remains of his realizations and transformations: and it is a good thing, the survivors of that period say in chorus, because his style was heavy and colossal even though it was functional. The monks called the stairway which led down from the dormitory to the church "the little fort." The style of his successor, Dom Guerric Baudet, is incontestably more sober and Cistercian. But we must be just and recognize that, as a whole, the restoration of the monastery was impressive, especially if we take into account the previous state of affairs and the sorely diminished resources of the abbey at that time. Furthermore, we can suppose that Dom Anselme was quite conscious of the limits of his architectural genius, if we go by what he wrote to Dom Alexis: "The Father Abbot of Cîteaux is planning transformations in his monastery. I took him to visit several interesting buildings in Belgium, then I brought him to Scourmont to show him what he ought not do!" He liked the "play of bricks" developed by Dom Bellot of Quarr Abbey, and had his faithful expert workman for it.

The year 1925 marked the 75th anniversary of the foundation of the Abbey. On this occasion the Father Abbot had a commemorative cross set up on the Wayères farm where the founding Fathers had settled in 1850. He also had a statue of Saint Joseph set up in the cloister, with an inscription graven in the marble officially expressing the monks' gratitude for his patronage. In 1926 he attacked the refectory. The old monks still remember how shabby this long, poorly-lighted room was, and how grim it looked in winter. After the refectory, it was the cloisters' turn and, in 1928, that of the chapter room. In 1929, he had a new wing built on the guest house, with a covered passageway connecting the two sections. In 1925, he had undertaken the gracious initiative of building a guesthouse for women. In 1934, he had the scriptorium and library enlarged, and a new novitiate shot up out of the earth in several weeks. In 1935, he renovated the old dormitory which with its worm-eaten floor and low ceiling was in bad need of renewal. To sum up, everything was renovated: the infirmary, the plumbing, the kitchen, the workshops, the enclosure. And in 1938, it was the church which was completely done over and which, if there had not been a Second World War, would have had an ambulatory.

In 1933, to guarantee solitude better for the Abbey, on the north and west sides of the monastery he acquired a few acres of fields and about 75 acres of woods. At the same time he took care to provide places of solitude and silence for the guests, in the line of thought of the Sovereign Pontiff who encouraged the development of "spiritual exercises" among lay people. Following his initiative, Scourmont still continues today to fulfill faithfully and simply this work which its fourth abbot assigned to it.

A builder with untiring hands and imagination, Dom le Bail left no rest to his mind either, nor to the minds of his monks. He incited his monks to apply themselves to study, seen as a development of *lectio divina*. He extolled affective theology, while at the same time insisting on a solid intellectual foundation. With this as goal, he acquired numerous valuable works and collections, thus creating a remarkable library for the use of his monks and those of the future. He had no desire to preserve the sad reputation of ignorant Trappists.

> The Cistercian monk should have zeal for studying the Cistercian Fathers. Oh! What an abundant source, both delicious and fitted to his needs. Ex-professo commentaries are not numerous, it is true, except on the *Song of Songs*; but their sermons, as well as all of their works, are nothing but texts from Holy

Scripture woven together. Saint Bernard speaks by Scripture. If the literal meaning is not always his dominant preoccupation, he does provide us with the advantage of very practical applications suited to monks of Cîteaux, in conformity with their state of soul, their rule and their type of life. The study of Holy Scripture according to the commentaries of Saint Bernard, William of Saint-Thierry, Guerric, Blessed Aelred should, at least once in the lifetime of every monk, extend over a long period. There he will find innumerable liturgical, ascetical and mystical applications.

At the end of his Rule, Saint Benedict refers his disciple to the Fathers in order to complete his spiritual instruction: "All of them point out the way which leads to highest perfection." Several of those whom he mentions should be preferred as masters of the spiritual life. One could not overdo in advising a monk to select among the works of the Fathers those which are most useful to him, and to reflect on those which are most edifying to him. Modern authors, of course, are easier to read and often more enjoyable. But—and a monk should not forget this—the Fathers, especially those who wrote about the monastic order: Saint Basil, Saint Jerome, Saint Augustine, Saint Gregory the Great, were raised up by God to be first of all "models for the flock, *forma gregis*," and then pastors. In a certain way one must apply to all these Fathers what Saint Bernard said of Saint Benedict: "*Pascit vita, pascit doctrina.*"

Dom Mabillon in his *Treatise on Studies* gave this lesson useful to every monk. And a Cistercian monk will approve without any reservations the famous Maurist's evident preference in his listing of the Fathers: "Of all the books the monks should or can read, after the Sacred Books there are none which can be more useful, or with which they ought to be more familiar, than the works of Saint Bernard. These works should be the most usual nourishment of their souls during their whole life, and they should never interrupt reading this great master of solitaries except to take them up again with more relish and avidity. When reading these works they will find everything they could hunt for elsewhere: solid teaching, charm, diversity, precision, brevity, fire, liveliness; and I do not know if one can find a person more particularly destined by God to reform the ways of the monastic life, or who has succeeded more than this

> great man." If all monks, according to what Mabillon says, should not put aside reading this great master of solitaries, what should we say about Cistercian monks! These monks should frequently read not only Saint Bernard, but the whole Cistercian school, especially the writers of the twelfth and thirteenth centuries. Already in the novitiate, the masters and doctrine of this school should be summarily presented to beginners. Once the monk's studies as a scholastic have been terminated, he will apply himself to developing this synthesis for himself. He should do this, because the Masters are his Fathers from whom he receives life. It is to them that we should expressly apply Saint Bernard's teaching on the role of paternity in the religious state: "This tree (which Saint Benedict was) bore fruit not only for those who lived in his era, but these fruits have been preserved until our time and continue to grow. He was certainly dear to both God and men; and if his presence was considered to be blessed in the past, like that of a number of other holy persons—who are forgotten today by everyone but God,—the memory of him still remains blessed today. Up until today, in fact, by the triple witness of his love, he feeds the Lord's flock with three kinds of fruit: he feeds it by his life, he feeds it by his teaching; he feeds it by his intercession."

Dom Anselme was fundamentally Benedictine. His frequent references to Mabillon show this, even though everyone knows that the eminent Maurist and Rancé were at sword's edge. All the same, as a true Cistercian Dom Le Bail recognized that the Cîteaux of the XIIth century was "a work that was pleasing to God," by the fact that it raised up doctors to teach a new generation of monks how to understand the doctrine of Saint Benedict, and to develop teaching of the Rule in its multiple applications. For the Father Abbot of Scourmont, the Cistercian school is in a certain way an irreplaceable commentary on the Benedictine Rule for Cistercian monks.

> The special interest which the Cistercian Fathers offer is that their writings are exclusively works of spirituality, and that most of them are directed directly to Cistercians, or at least to monks who follow the Rule of Saint Benedict. So they are perfectly cut out to be our guides. They had the grace; they had

> the experience; they acquired the knowledge. So we should go to them: we must follow them, otherwise we will fall by the wayside, or not possess fully the spirit of our vocation. The monk will study them. Just as the Fathers did, they will select the authors and treatises which suit them best. If the monk follows Mabillon's advice never to abandon these books, during the course of his life he will arrive at a good knowledge of his Cistercian school, and will no doubt also reap a good harvest.

In 1928 two student-monks who had graduated from universities in Rome returned to Scourmont. Others followed them, and it continued that way for years. The Father Abbot wanted to have a group of qualified professors for his monastery. There can no doubt be excellent formators without degrees. Nevertheless, as he saw it, a diploma remained a guaranty of competence and a cultivated mind. He dreamed of such university formation for the majority of the monks, in order to assure a high intellectual level for the whole community.

In the public reading in the refectory—"*cibus cibo melior*" (better food than the meal)—, the Father Abbot preferred historical books; whereas for the reading before Compline he had the monks read works of spirituality or extracts from works of the Fathers of the Church, while secretly desiring readings from the Cistercian Fathers. But at that time the existing translations left much to be desired, so that their contents risked being undervalued. At the beginning of Lent, it sometimes happened that certain monks received for their Lenten reading a volume of Migne's patrology, with the invitation to make a polished and accurate translation of it. As he pointed out to them, this was an efficacious way to keep from dozing in the scriptorium in the morning.

In his daily Chapters Dom Anselme lavished his sons with carefully structured instructions rich in doctrine. He commented on the Rule of Saint Benedict in a continuous way and liked to refer to the *Summa* of Saint Thomas Aquinas to elucidate one or another point of doctrine, for example, interpreting Chapter 2 of the Rule "On the qualities that an Abbot should have" (*Qualis debeat Abbas esse*) in the light of the virtue of prudence.

For his Sunday Chapters, he based what he said on the liturgical texts, drawing up powerful syntheses on the Mysteries of the Incarnation, the Redemption, the Church and the Sacraments.

He even profited from the time for peeling potatoes to offer his monks a little snack (*"collation"*), in this case, a little conference on the spot. Here is one of them dating from 1939 that has come down to us. It shows his humor which apparently no one could resist:

> A snack while my sons are peeling potatoes, apples, pears, chicory, turnips and other roots:
>
>> Rare, but permitted, the spiritual snack was a means of edification for the Desert Fathers, for Saint Benedict, at Rievaulx when Saint Aelred was abbot, at Stella under Isaac while grub was being prepared and at La Trappe under Rancé. And so, at Scourmont, where everyone is a master—a master in thinking—the snack can be a means of edification: *"loqui et docere magistrum condecet"* . . . it is for the master to speak and teach (R.B. VI).
>
> With this purpose, having called upon the holy name of God, and without consulting the Chapter, we raise the vegetable-preparers to the dignity and function of thought-preparers.

These remarks were followed by an outline of what he wanted to say during a half-hour of preparing vegetables. It is a question of the *Visio Dei in creaturis*, "The Vision of God in his creatures" according to Saint Edmond of Canterbury in his *"Speculum Ecclesiae"*:

> We can see the *"Potestas Dei* . . . the Power of God" in all his creatures and in their multitude, through the four dimensions: height, depth, length and broadness.
>
> We can see the *"Sapientia Dei* . . . the wisdom of God" in all its beauty and in its multiple manifestations, that of quite simply being; that of being and living; that of being and feeling; that of being and living, feeling and understanding.
>
> We can see the *"Bonitas Dei* . . . God's goodness," thanks to the usefulness of his works to us. When they make us happy

> they are useful in helping and leading us. When they put us to the test, they are useful in instructing and purifying us.
>
> Therefore, my brothers, *"Te Deum laudamus"*: let us praise God for his Powerfulness, let us adore Him for his Wisdom, and let us glorify Him for his Goodness.

Dom Anselme's humor, in its numerous and various forms, was never unwarranted or frivolous. It was always aimed at opening up the intellect and heart. Once it assumed astonishing dimensions with regard to what is sacred when, on September 7, 1925, before the first Vespers of the Nativity of the Blessed Virgin, the Father Abbot went to the jubé with his ministers and acolytes, and turning towards the new organ declaimed the following, worthy of being put in an anthology:

> Grand organ of Scourmont, I solemnly command you, in the name of God the Father, Creator and Principle of all harmony; in the name of God the Son, the Word, and Praise, form of all praise, in the name of the Holy Spirit, the Breath which creates and renews everything on earth; in the name of Our Lady who, when she sang the *Magnificat*, gave rise to the choirs of the new Testament; in the name of Saint Bernard, the Master who laid down the rules for Cistercian chant; in the name of the Authority given to me by the Catholic Church in this church of Scourmont, over souls and things, I solemnly command you to remain what you ought to be, and to attain the goal for which you have been intended, built and tuned.
>
> And I solemnly command you to be, in our church, the co-worker of the work of God.
>
> The Work of God accomplished on earth by men, by the monastic choir of this church, is the clear knowledge of God's greatness, admiration, thanksgiving, supplication. So that on earth man alone—as an intelligent being with a loving heart—can be God's chorister, "Grand Organ," you can be his coadjutor; you should be only his coadjutor.
>
> Coadjutor of our monastic Office, I solemnly command you: always remain the servant who does not crush by the brutal power of your 17 stops and 973 voices the more weak but more intelligent and loving voice of your master, the choir of

> Notre-Dame de Scourmont. Be its humble coadjutor who helps the soul to humble itself in adoration; be the coadjutor who carries thanksgiving up to God's throne on your heavenly voices. Be the sober and gentle helper of the penitent soul who sighs, of the poor soul who entreats. "Grand organ," I solemnly command: always remain the helper of the Work of God. May God, through you, renew for the choir of Notre-Dame de Scourmont the theophany of the prophet Elias on Mount Sinai. May storm winds which tear out mountains and break up rocks never come forth from you: God is not in a whirlwind. Do not pretend to imitate the earthquake that the Prophet then heard: God is not in violent agitation. By your sweet and light harmony, like the murmuring of a soft breeze which Elias heard at last, reveal the Lord to our souls.
>
> If you are not a coadjutor in this church, may the flames of fire consume your worthless tin. So be it! So be it!

But is it true that the head and hands of this man were so immune to fatigue? During these years of intense activity, he wrote to his aunt:

> You were very right to complain about my silence. It exceeds all limits. My responsibilities occupy me completely. And the more one advances in age, the more this responsibility becomes overburdening. Generally speaking, I am well, except that I suffer from frequent and painful migraines.

And in a collective letter to his family:

> During the last three years I have put on weight. And yet, I fast almost every day of the year. But I feel that I am getting old, I am having trouble with my heart. It is my portly figure which is the cause.

When he wrote these lines Dom Anselme had hardly begun his 48th year. But the wear and tear were beginning to show, in spite of his intense energy. His monks began to notice it a little bit in his instructions during morning Chapter: although the way he spoke was always lively and his teaching enjoyable, its form began to show less careful preparation. A struggle against death was beginning to take place in his physical organism. It would last a long time, more than twenty years.

22

Go out, all right, but without miter and crozier

During the twenty years between the two wars, the Father Abbot had a profound influence not only on his community, but also on the Order and beyond. A studious man, he published very little of his work, but unsparingly shared an abundant oral teaching, principally on the subject of Benedictine and Cistercian spirituality.

He was listened to at the General Chapter. From 1928 on he was an active member of the Liturgy Commission, and in 1936 became secretary of this Commission and also of the Commission for the Menology. Thanks to his incentives these two Commissions were remarkably active, as the "Acts of the Commission of Liturgy" shows. Among Dom Anselme's personal achievements in the Commission were the "Ceremonial for the manner in which to receive the Sisters" and the "Ceremonial for Abbots."

This subject of reform of the Cistercian liturgy brings us back once again to the correspondence he kept up with Dom Alexis Presse, who also had his little ideas on the question, as well as—and especially—some big ideas. Dom Anselme humbly gave him his confidence, but he also asked him to be more patient and less outspoken about them. Here are several passages taken at random from letters Dom Le Bail wrote to Dom Presse. They reveal his good sense and also his sense of humor:

> Thank you for all the notes you sent me. I shared with you some little questions which show you how much I am a novice-

> monk and novice-Abbot with regard to this subject. I like to learn from good masters, and among them, the Reverend Fathers of our Generalate: they possess sanctity, knowledge, and especially, leisure.
>
> I was very happy to see your pages on the use of Pontificals. I recognize the value of your principle concerning the integrity of the primitive Rite, including, if you really want it that way, exclusion of carpets and return to iron candlesticks, while leaving the possibility for anyone who wants to use carpets to do so; the principle still remains. Your arguments seem to me to be well backed up by documents and very concise. But I admit to you that I am more interested in the soul of the liturgy than in the rubrics. I do not have your absolute vision: "Yes-Yes: no-no." In all of that I would be tempted to add a sly remark, something like this: "In surplice or cowl, the world keeps rolling along."
>
> In spite of your fixed ideas—as you yourself realize they are—I would not be displeased if you would draw up a notice for the General Chapter. I would like to have your collaboration, and even more than collaboration: it is you who should draw up the proposals. Very eminent Father, most high doctor, I prostrate myself before the white peak of Tamié and before your crowned personage.

It was also due to Dom Anselme's initiative and thanks to his encouragement—a rare attitude at that time in Trappist monasteries—that several of his monks undertook intellectual study projects and published them: Father Benoît Attout, Dom Godefroid Bélorgey, Father Colomban Bock, Father Joseph Canivez, Father Hugh Clément, Father Jean-Chrysostome Daumont, Father Tiburce Grimaud, Father Camille Hontoir, Father Idesbald Huille, Father Edmond Jacquemin, Father Paul Stevens. All these publications were listed in a work signed by Dom Le Bail and Father Bock, *Un siècle de vie monastique, Abbaye N.-D. de Scourmont* (1950, pages 119–129).

It is equally important to say something about Dom Anselme as a lecturer and retreat master, because this was an area of activity difficult for him to manage to fit in, as is the case for many abbots both yesterday and today. Once again, it is in his correspondence with his dear friend Alexis Presse that we discover his personal struggle. His lucidity and honesty are faultless.

> I receive more and more bitter remarks from my monks who reproach me for going out too much. They are right, and by these remarks they show me their attachment. And in spite of the brake I want to put on my outside engagements, there are still too many of them. But you know how that works: At first you are left in your corner and you observe enclosure very well; then you meet someone who persuades you to go out. "Oh, it's only for this one time," you tell yourself. So you go out and you meet two other people, and you are booked twice. You go out twice and you accept four engagements. The cogwheels are turning, and you are completely caught in them. So one becomes an Abbot for the outside, and one gives as an excuse making the monastery known. One is no longer anything but a gyrovague. What a terrible thing! Today I am making the resolution not to go out except to preach and to preside Confirmations as a service to the diocese, without showing off my miter or crozier.
>
> I have spoken to you about my resolutions. During this month of August I am sad because I let myself be caught three times to preach a retreat. A three weeks absence! When I promised, I could not foresee that they would come one after the other and during the same month!
>
> These months of April–June, I am bothered about my going out: twelve times! I promise too easily, and finally I am too involved. What consoles me is that I go out only to preach, and I refuse when I am asked to appear in miter and with a crozier.

Unfortunately we will never be the little mouse who might have heard Dom Anselme preach. We can suppose that his sermons were savory, when we read the list of communities and places where he was invited and esteemed.

He preached retreats for the Benedictine communities at Maredsous, Mont-César and Saint-André de Bruges; for the Bernardines of Blandain; for the Carmelites of Compiègne; for the Trappists of Rochefort and Bonnecombe; for the Trappistines of Soleilmont and Chimay; for the community of Mont-Vierge at Wépion; at Laval, Ollignies, Audregnies, Bonsecours. He gave lectures on the Cistercian writers at Sept-Fons, Orval, Mont-des-Cats and Cîteaux.

Sister Bernard of Chimay left us this account:

> Dom Anselme preached our retreat. Two instructions each day. No confessions. He left those to a Jesuit Father who was present in the house. He did the Compline reading himself. He developed the Marian theme: "Live in presence of the Blessed Virgin." He said that she is here with us, but not in the same way as the Father who is present everywhere, nor in the way Christ is in the Eucharist, nor in the way of the Spirit who flutters about above us. Dom Anselme then stretched out his arms, flapped his hands, rocked on his chair, imitating an angel flying around. He told us that he did not know how Mary is present to us, but he assured us of her presence as if he was able to see Our Lady. At the same time he told us that Mary is not in any place. About the time of the Beauraing apparitions, it happened that the monk who was driving him, said: "Reverend Father, we will go by Beauraing." Dom Anselme answered: "That's right;. we will go by Beauraing." When they arrived at Beauraing, the young monk opened the car door and said: "Reverend Father, here we are at Beauraing; would you like to get out?" Dom Anselme answered: "Brother, I accepted that we go by Beauraing, nothing more. Get back in the car: for us, Our Lady is in our cloister." To consecrate oneself to Mary, he said, is simply to be her servants and to accept her orders as being our duties. And during his instructions he forbad us to take notes. He said: "It is not writing that you must do, but doing." He spoke to us about nothing but the Rule of Saint Benedict.

We can say, however, that over and above his teaching Dom Anselme fascinated his listeners, because they saw in him a man with no complexes or inhibitions; an Abbot without any arrogance, the witness of a monastery where there was no cold self-centeredness, a wise adviser and a merciful priest.

23

Rewarded audacity: *Collectanea*

During the 1924 General Chapter Father Abbot Anselme Le Bail presented an audacious project: publication of a Collection of Cistercian works and, in a larger view, a connecting link among the existing monasteries. The Collection would consist of three series: 1. Cistercian ascesis and mysticism: the original text, a French translation with an introduction, and commentaries on the texts drawn from the spirituality of the Cistercian Fathers from the XIIth until the XVth century. 2. A Cistercian history, including biographies of Cistercian Blessed, and monographs on monasteries. 3. Cistercian Law relative to discipline and liturgy.

The presentation of the project was far from being vague and theoretical, because for years Dom Anselme had been accumulating thousands of pages of notes from his reading. In 1923, he had already begun—and he amused himself a bit with this—to make bound copies, in his handwriting of course, of possible volumes.

The material of the first volume included a precise bibliography of Cistercian authors—most of them renowned but unknown to most monks at that time—supported by references to volumes of *Latin Patrology*. What he turned up is impressive: Saint Bernard; William of Saint-Thierry; Saint Amadeus of Lausanne; Blessed Aelred; Serlon; Isaac of Stella; Hugh, Abbot of Trois-Fontaines; Fastrède, Abbot of Cambron, Clairvaux, Cîteaux; Gilbert of Hoyland; Thomas; Nicholas of Clairvaux; Philippe, Abbot of Aumône; Pierre Monoculus, 8e Abbot of Clairvaux; Henry, Abbot of Clairvaux and Cardinal of Albano; Geoffrey of Auxerre; Blessed

Guerric of Igny; Geoffrey of Péronne, Prior of Clairvaux; Peter of Roye, a novice at Clairvaux; Arnulphe of Boheries; Elias of Coxyde, Abbot of Dunes; Adam of Perseigne; Gonthier; Hélinand of Froidmont; Caesarius of Heisterbach. All of these were Cistercians between 1090 and 1240.

A second volume, on the three masters of Cîteaux, was drawn up in great detail. It contained: Chapter 1, The preparation of Cîteaux, that is to say, first of all a spiritual portrait of Robert, Albéric and Stephen; next, an analysis of the crisis at Molesmes; and lastly, the foundation of the "New Monastery." Dom Anselme did not relate banal details. Thanks to the reading he had done, he dared to express his own interpretation of the facts:

> During its first twenty years of existence, the Abbey of Molesmes prospered calmly, and nothing seems to have troubled the brothers' peace. The abbey was so fervent that two of its monks, Guérin and Guy, were sent to make a new foundation in the Alps. And yet, suddenly a crisis arose, which has traditionally been attributed to decadence in the Abbey. To say that it came about because of this, however, seems to be too rapid a judgment and too easy, since it was a question of a community which had been in existence for only twenty years and whose founders were still present and in charge. Its cause seems to have been a profound divergence between two ways of perceiving things, and therefore between two groups in the community. This divergence, furthermore, seems normal in a young foundation whose monks had been exposed to different spiritual influences before they entered the monastery, as well as to a variety of different disciplinary rules: some were attached to the customs of Cluny which were held in esteem at that time; others, and particularly the Superiors, wanted a life style that was more in keeping with the simplicity of Saint Benedict's Rule. In the *Exordium Magnum* there is evidence that during the morning Chapters, reading the Rule often stirred up troubled waters and gave rise to commentaries comparing the Cluniac style at Molesmes with Benedictine sobriety. It was from Alberic that the idea of a reform came. And Stephen, with his practical character, had the merit of having suggested the establishment of a new monastery. As for Robert, who was

> audacious but also saddened by the division in the community, he disappeared for a while to Haux, a small farm which depended on the Abbey. That was all that was needed for the monks who had Cluniac leanings to persecute their brothers who had Benedictine tendencies. So it was that 21 monks, following Robert, Alberic and Stephen, left Molesmes for Cîteaux, the "New Monastery."

Chapter II analyzed the *"Exordium Cistercii"*; Chapter III, the *"Carta caritatis."* In his conclusion, Dom Anselme gave an interpretation of the Cîteaux reform, one which was neither romantic, nor partisan, nor sociological, but objectively theological, and even Thomist:

> This base of this new School was founded on this primordial truth: God is pleased to communicate himself to men through secondary causes, through creatures or one single creature. This creature communicates to men—now by a reminder of revealed truth, now by the practice of this truth—a way of perfection adapted to a certain context of living, at a given epoch, to specific souls. And since this creature is God's instrument, his way is sacred and consequently should not be transgressed or modified by those to whom it is addressed. Such was the doctrine of the founders of Cîteaux; and such would be the theological justification given to it by Saint Thomas Aquinas and, with him, the whole Church. (Cf. *Summa Theologica* IIa,IIae, q.104, art.1).
>
> To men of the whole world were sent Abraham, Moses, David, the great Prophets, and finally Our Lord Jesus Christ, who always referred to the Law and to the requirements of the Covenant. In the Church there were men sent at a precise epoch and for particular Christians: Saint Benedict was one such man, *"organum Spiritus Sancti,"* sent to speak to monks of all times, and precisely for monks of the XIIth century and for the founders of Cîteaux who had a "sacred" veneration for him. The fact that at a certain time they deviated from this—and the *Exordium* speaks of "sacrilegious" transgression—should not be at all surprising to us. *"Hodie, si vocem eius audieritis, nolite obdurare corda vestra"—"Today, if you hear his voice, do not harden your hearts."* Here, in this spirit of faith, God's voice and Saint Benedict's voice are one. *"Regulae vestigiis sunt adaequati et confor-*

> *mati,"* says the *Exordium*: the new monks are simply harmonized, adjusted and faithful to the ways proposed by the Benedictine Rule.

The last chapter is devoted to analysis and research concerning the meaning of the *"Consuetudines,"* the *"Instituta Capituli"* and the *"Usus Conversorum"* of the new Cîteaux. Dom Anselme's conclusion consists of admiration for the wisdom of the Cistercian founders who, realizing very well how pride and egoism can lead people astray, proposed to monks a school of service of the Lord, so that all together and individually they could find simple and practical means of conforming themselves to God's will.

A third book, more voluminous than the preceding—112 quarto in tightly squeezed handwriting—is consecrated to Saint Bernard. There Dom Anselme mixed together an unimaginable number of morsels of information, notes and reflections. It would be tedious to quote the 10 Chapters and their numerous paragraphs. Let us content ourselves simply with Dom Anselme's conclusion:

> The most perfect conclusion of the life and work of Saint Bernard was given us, long ago, by one of the most exquisite and authentic painters of the Italian renaissance: Fra Angelico. In his painting of the Crucifixion, at the foot of the cross he placed the principal bright lights of the monastic Order. Saint Bernard is represented there clasping a book to his breast—would it not be the *Song of Songs*?—and fixing his eyes on Jesus on the cross: in his gaze there is something inexpressibly tender, grave and mysterious, which brings out and portrays the saint's whole soul in an infinitely better way than the study—necessarily a bit cold and objective—which we have presented here. Because when he crossed the threshold of Cîteaux he had no other wish than to be a monk, a man who loves God.

Briefly, when Dom Anselme presented his extraordinary project at the 1924 General Chapter, it was by no means theoretical: the Father Abbot already had everything in his head and in his notes. The abbots of the Order listened to him attentively and with interest. Behind the scenes, however, there was talk of megalomania, like—it was insinuated—his building a new study room at Scourmont. Dom Anselme did not insist. For him, what was important was that the idea had been launched. Once again he showed that he was humble and patient. He wrote to his friend Dom Alexis Presse:

> Ignorant people like me are always audacious when they undertake something. But their failure to succeed can stir up competent people and incite them to act without waiting until their project is perfect . . . and death arrives.

When he returned to Scourmont Dom Anselme worked day and night, and encouraged his monks to do research. He read, took notes, composed essays, nourished his community with his findings and preached retreats. The impulse had been given, at Scourmont and in other Cistercian communities. The letters he received from other Trappist Abbeys where he preached retreats show this, like a refrain: "You have given us the taste to know our Cistercian Fathers. Here, we are applying ourselves to that. Thank you!"

It would take ten years before the first issue of "*Collectanea Ordinis Cisterciensium Reformatorum*" would be published, in April, 1934, by Westmalle's printing shop. The preface was entrusted to Dom Herman Joseph Smets, Abbot General. Its contents, even though still a bit timid, could not but make Dom Anselme happy.

> *Collectanea* refuses a priori any and all pretension to be erudite. Its intention is in no way publication of a "learned Review," even if it will instruct our religious concerning the branches of sacred knowledge that are of direct interest to them, as for example: Cistercian spirituality, liturgical questions and our particular law. Even these teachings, however, far from exposing their authors to the danger of vain showing-off of their intellectual capacities, or leading them into vain polemics, will bear the stamp of scrupulous care to help souls to progress in the love of God.

Renouncing henceforth the slogan "*scientia inflat*," the Abbot General quoted Saint Bernard verbatim: "*Scientia sine caritat inflat. Caritas sine scientia errat. Caritas cum scientia aedificat.*" Dom Anselme certainly agreed. It was even the battle he had been waging for years: knowledge puffs up a person with pride if it is not accompanied by the love of Charity. But Charity, if it is not accompanied by knowledge, goes adrift. What builds up a community, in fact, is the meeting of love and intelligence.

The first issue, as well as those which followed, did not simply translate vaguely Dom Le Bail's first intuition; it was a concrete application of the propositions set forth in 1924. We find there, in fact, an article by Dom Chautard, Abbot of Sept-Fons, on "The Rule of Saint Benedict, illustrated by Saint Bernard";—an article by Dom Alexis Presse, Abbot of Tamié, on "Saint Stephen Harding";—chronicles on several Cistercian Abbeys;—and a "Bibliography of Saint Stephen Harding," signed by the monks of Chimay. Below this signature, the brother librarian at Scourmont wrote in pencil: actually, Dom Anselme Le Bail.

We can well understand Dom Anselme's discretion: suspected of intellectual tendencies by the majority of Abbots of the opposite tendency, he avoided having his name appear too soon and too often in the periodical. But he obtained that the editor would be a monk of Scourmont, Father Camille Hontoir. This is as much as saying that *Collectanea* was entrusted to the monks of Chimay, for the greatest good of the magazine. The year of Father Camille's death, the author of his biographical notice well wrote in the 1958 *Collectanea*: "If we would have to pinpoint Father Camille's character, or describe his personality, it seems to me that we could present him as a Christian humanist par excellence who, after knowing and appreciating men and having studied and possessed sciences and philosophy, made a personal synthesis of all these values and measured how relative they were before the holiness of God."

Father Camille himself expressed his thought about the way he saw his function as editor of *Collectanea*. We can recognize there Dom Le Bail's inspiration, faithfully presented:

> Monastic souls have an intense need to be instructed in the things of God: in the very special form of their vocation, it is necessary for them to receive a teaching proper to their state;

and even more, besides the knowledge of the privileged means of tending toward perfection which constitute the religious state in general, a knowledge of the means proper to the Order, and which express the spirit of the Order, is needed.

24

Scourmont to the rescue of Soleilmont

Notre-Dame de Soleilmont Abbey, located in the diocese of Tournai in Belgium—the same diocese the Trappist monastery of Scourmont belongs to—is the home of a community of Cistercian nuns of the Strict Observance. The monastery, built in 1973, is not far from its ancient buildings destroyed by fire in 1963. Only a few kilometres separate Soleilmont from Scourmont, located in French-speaking Wallonia. These two bonds—geographical and linguistic—explain the "incident" which follows. In the beginning, however, there was perfect understanding between the community of Soleilmont and Dom Anselme, who in 1919 accepted with joy and enthusiasm to introduce the nuns' request for aggregation to the Order of the Strict Observance.

Soleilmont has a long, laborious history which is worth knowing. Dom Anselme left us an account of it, written in his ornate style. We have before our eyes a Visitation Card for the year 1919, written by Dom Le Bail in elegant calligraphy on exquisite paper. It must have given Dom Anselme's mind and heart a real treat while he was writing it. We are not going to resist the temptation to transcribe it here:

> We, Brother Anselme Le Bail, Abbot of Notre-Dame de Saint Joseph at Forges-lez-Chimay, in the diocese of Tournai, making the regular Visitation at the Venerable Abbey of Notre-Dame de Soleilmont, to resume a tradition begun in the year 1237 by the Abbots of Villers, Val Saint-Lambert and Aulne, and interrupted in 1789, acting in this visit by the authorization of His Grandeur Monsignor Crooy, bishop and superior of this place,

without however a mission of the General Chapter of the Order, but moved by charity with regard to this community and by zeal to introduce it, by its reform, to the fullness of the observances and customs of Cîteaux, we have found under the guidance of Dame Marie, the very worthy Prioress, seven choir religious, six choir novices, eleven lay sisters, one lay novice, making twenty-six persons all together.

On June 11, the Wednesday of the octave of Pentecost, after celebrating Mass we proceeded to opening the visitation by an exhortation on the Cistercian life, which we completed on this same day; the next day we gave five instructions on Cistercian occupations and observances; the following days we received each of the nuns privately, and even each of the lay sisters and each novice, each of whom presented herself spontaneously. Finally, on June 15, on the solemn feast of the Most Blessed Trinity, we concluded the visitation with the reading of the following visitation card:

My Reverend Mothers, my dear sisters,

Before the zeal which inspires you and urges you to resume the practice of the Rule of Saint Benedict according to the institutions of Cîteaux after a period during which they had been put aside, we have wanted to put this spirit to the test—according to the advice given in Scripture—and we have found its significance and value, we believe, in the history of your monastery.

On March 23, 1239, Pope Gregory IX, of glorious memory, by according to Notre-Dame de Soleilmont a bull of confirmation, decreed and mandated that the monastic order according to the Rule of Saint Benedict and the Institutions of Cîteaux would be inviolably observed there forever "*Statuentes ut ordo monasticus . . . perpetuis ibidem temporibus inviolabiliter observetur.*"

Time has passed since then; these words of the Vicar of Christ have not passed. God's Spirit has taken care of reminding you of them and of bringing them to realization in your community in spite of and contrary to the vicissitudes of human weakness. The Rule of Saint Benedict was practised here already in 1088. And just as at Monte Casino it brought about the ruin of the altars of Venus, here it did away with the cult of the Sun on a neighbouring mountain, named for this reason *Soleil-Mont*.

Two centuries passed, and the Benedictine nuns died in decadence with regard to their Rule. Soleilmont, however, did not die. By a decision of the General Chapter of the Order of Cîteaux in 1237, the Cistercian nuns of Flines, of the filiation of Clairvaux, came to make the Rule of Saint Benedict flourish again, promising to observe it inviolably forever: this was the first Resurrection of Soleilmont.

Two centuries went by, however, and the Rule seems to have been transgressed in this community to the point that the General Chapter of 1413 decreed that the abbess and religious of this place should abandon their monastery: the perpetuity asked by Gregory IX was going to collapse. But no, the Spirit of God breathed into the hearts of the religious and there was a renewal of zeal for the Rule. According to the *Chronicle*, like prodigal children they threw themselves at the feet of Dom Godefroid, Abbot of Aulne and their Father Immediate, imploring his help with tears and groans and begging him to have pity on them. They made a thousand protests and promises to live in conformity with their religious vows in the future. "Dame Marie d'Alvet immediately undertook a reform. And toward the end of 1414, Dame Marie de Senzeilles, of the illustrious family of that name and a religious of Soleilmont, was elected abbess and with vigorous courage restored the original regular life and monastic discipline in all its fervor. Gregory IX's order was preserved: at Soleilmont the Rule of Saint Benedict remained inviolable forever: "*perpetuis ibidem temporibus inviolabiliter observetur.*" This was Soleilmont's second Resurrection.

Time went on. The French Revolution, which in general had done away with the monasteries in these regions, found the Cistercian nuns of Soleilmont securely and unconquerably attached to their place and to the Rule. To the solicitations of the commissaries of the Revolution who asked them to abandon their property and this Rule, Dame Scholastica Daivier, the Abbess, replied with an energetic "never," echoed by a chorus of twenty religious backing her up in saying "never." In 1797, they were obliged to yield to force; but in their place of refuge at Farciennes the Rule was maintained intact. Furthermore, they were able to go back to Soleilmont in 1802. Dame Davier gave the reason for this when, as she was dying, she left to her daughters as a standing order the words of Gregory

IX: keep the Rule inviolably, and hold good at Soleilmont: "*ibidem . . . inviolabiliter.*"

This was Soleilmont's third Resurrection.

And finally, in our time, after almost a century, and especially since 1863 when the community of Soleilmont seemed to be oriented forever toward teaching and had put aside almost all the observances of Cîteaux, the Holy Spirit continued to watch over them so that the words of the Vicar of Christ, spoken seven centuries before, would not be abandoned. By inspiration of the Spirit combined with the initiative of Dame Xavier, the prioress, and Messire Brohée, the discreet president of the Seminary Leo XIII in Louvain, who during the war had become chaplain at Soleilmont because of his devotion for the monastic life; and finally, with the authorization of his Grandeur Monseigneur Amédée Crooy, bishop of Tournai, zeal for the Rule of Saint Benedict according to the Institutions of Cîteaux germinated and flowered in the hearts of the nuns and sisters, echoing their mothers of the XIIth, XVth, XVIIIth centuries, always coming back to the order of the Vicar of Christ: observe the Rule inviolably and perpetually in the same place, Soleilmont "*Statuentes un ordo monasticus . . . perpetuis ibidem temporibus inviolabiliter observetur.*" This was Soleilmont's fourth Resurrection.

Reverend Mothers, my dear Sisters,

Does this admirable history of your abbey not prove that your spirit and project of Reform come from God? You are the daughters of the saints of Soleilmont, guardians of the words of Gregory IX. You must be vigilant so as not to let what has been entrusted to you die out, and not to deviate from what you have inherited. In order to do that, you should be attentive first of all to acquiring and developing in yourselves the Cistercian spirit: the Cistercian spirit, I am saying, not only Cistercian observances. The latter are only the body of a Cistercian; the former is the soul. Without the soul, the human body is a cadaver; without the Cistercian spirit, the observances are reduced to Pharisaism. The Cistercian spirit consists in orienting one's life solely to the service of Our Lord Jesus Christ by prayer and penance. It is the Christian life in its full flowering, without any doubt; but there is more, applying one's whole being to God alone, to the exclusion of apostolic activity toward souls outside. To be alone with God alone, to love and expiate: that is the Cistercian soul, in its deepest sense. So you must develop this contemplative spirit, that is to say, you must train your soul to remain habitually in the presence of God, in union with Our Lord Jesus Christ, to praise Him, pray to Him, in imitation of the first hierarchy of Angels, Thrones, Cherubim and Seraphim. Here, formation should be conducted with ardent and persevering solicitude. A soul is formed to the contemplative life by the practice of prayer, by times devoted frequently to prayer; but also by application of the spirit to know God so as to love Him. The Cistercian worthy of this name is an enlightened soul. In her reading, she seeks to penetrate the things of God: God's life in itself; God's works in the Incarnation, Redemption and in the Church. In one word, Christian doctrine is the sun which enlightens and warms the soul. Enlightened concerning the works of God because she is a contemplative, the Cistercian should also be enlightened about expiation because she is a penitent. She should be instructed about the spirit of penance which is above all consciousness of our nothingness and human misery, and which inclines the heart to lower itself before God in full dependence and to give up everything, to abandon one's whole being, to expiate, to suffer. This is the meaning of Our Father Saint Bernard's words explaining the penitential goal of our Order: "Our Order," he said, "is humility and abjection." In seeking these two goals in her life, the religious of Cîteaux finds an incentive in the thought that she is not working for her salvation and sanctification alone, but also for the Church. She, too, has her place and active role in the mystical Body of Christ; she, too, is a soldier of Christ, combating for Him, rendering Him for the glory of His Father and for the salvation of souls the two services of prayer and penance: such is the Cistercian spirit. The Cistercian works should be the exterior expression of it. The Cistercian works are the Divine Office, sacred reading, manual work. In order to devote herself to them efficaciously, the religious needs favorable surroundings: she should love solitude, be attached to the place and to her sisters "*amator loci et fratrum*," be recollected in silence: all that, she owes and wants in order to be alone with God alone, according to the meaning of the name of "*moniale*" that she bears in the Church. In addition, she has the same zeal for the observances: poverty, the regular life, fasting, abstinence, vigils, knowing that the observances are what gives strength to her life. They are the discipline of the monastic army. What is more, in order to be a perfect Cistercian in all this the religious ought to know the value of each of her duties. She wants to serve her Master Jesus Christ with intelligence. The Divine Office, the "*opus Dei*," to which she should prefer nothing else, occupies the greatest place in her activities: she understands the liturgy, she familiarizes herself with the meaning of the texts in the Office, with the chant and the liturgical year, and is attentive to everything which could favor and develop her contemplative life and her love for God, instead of letting herself slide into routine. In this summary of the Cistercian life the Father Abbot Visitor recommends more especially to the solicitude of the Reverend Mothers and dear Sisters of the community of Soleilmont: 1: Knowledge of the Cistercian spirit, to be transmitted and acquired by instructions and by good choice of what is to be read in public before Compline and in the refectory, as well as in private reading. 2: Zeal for knowledge and practice of the liturgical life. 3: Solicitude to understand and observe the law of Cistercian silence, the observance the most apt to assure in the Order a spirit of prayer and penitence, the very goals of the Cistercian life.

If you do these things, the Cistercian renewal which you have begun and which has attained such great perfection will reach its full-flowering. You will then have come to realize the meaning of the Charter of your foundation in 1239, which should remain a motto of this community: observe the monastic order according to the Rule of Saint Benedict and the Institutions of Cîteaux, here at Soleilmont, inviolably and perpetually.

And the present card will be read in the Chapter room, after Prime, on Saturdays of Ember Days.

Given in the Abbey of Our Lady of Soleilmont, the 15th day of June, 1919, on the solemnity of the Most Holy Trinity.

The next year, 1920, Dom Anselme made the regular Visitation and observed that "the year has been good for affiliation to Cîteaux":

This year the Order of Cistercians of the Strict observance has spoken and concluded that you are one of theirs. It has given

> you the right to call yourselves "Cistercians of the Strict Observance." It has made you participants of all its spiritual goods. One could not give more to a community making its first petition. But from now on you can be assured that the next General Chapter will crown your way upward: the Order of Cistercians of the Strict Observance will juridically aggregate you to itself, with all the resulting rights and obligations.

This was done during the 1921 General Chapter. Dom Anselme, who was delayed in Congo, was not present. Designation of a Father Immediate for Soleilmont was consequently left open. While Dom Anselme was still in Congo, he received a letter Dom Norbert wrote to him from Rome. It led him to believe that this matter was not going to be simple:

> At the General Chapter I explained that a Father Immediate could be appointed during your absence, and that I knew that you preferred not to be the Father Immediate of Soleilmont. Nevertheless, by deference it was decided to await your return. The Father Abbot Hermann of Westmalle finds himself in a delicate situation. He knows that if you are not appointed Soleilmont would prefer him to Dom Henry, the Abbot of Rochefort, who would be willing to accept even though his community would not like it: he is waiting to be able to say that he has been obliged to accept.

When he came back from Congo in February, 1922, Dom Anselme wrote to Soleilmont on March 6:

> Reverend Mother, when I returned from Africa all the news and all the things about Soleilmont touched me deeply: the filiation had not been determined, whereas I believed that it had been decided: a personal letter had informed me of it; Dame Xavier died, that touched me, too, because I did not expect it; lastly, there is a new Prioress, and it is you, Your Reverence. I do not pity you too much, because things are going very well at Soleilmont and everything indicates that God is giving you a hand and making the community prosper. This means that the duties of the Superior are easier to bear. May God give you wisdom. As concerns the affiliation, insofar as

that depends on me, the decision will soon be forthcoming. I believed that the General Chapter would decide it without me. Precisely, I did not want the decision to come from me, but from the General Chapter, spontaneously. In any case, my Reverend Mother, this decision can not depend on congeniality or indifference on my part. From the point of view of my sentiments and affection for Soleilmont, I will not change: I admire Soleilmont for its reform, for its zeal for what is Cistercian; I love Soleilmont because it represents the continuity of our Order in Belgium for centuries. If that is all that one needs to be a Father Immediate, I am yours in my heart. And if I am not, these same sentiments will remain, and will manifest themselves by solicitude and devotedness. For the time being this attachment to Soleilmont means that if for your affiliation in the Order it would be necessary for Chimay to take you under its direction, and that no other house can be found to do so, I would do it unhesitatingly for this one single reason: that I want you to be in the Order. But this devotedness on our part is not necessary. Other houses are willing and able to assume the paternity. So the question comes back to weighing the advantages on both sides. What advantages can Soleilmont expect from Chimay and not from another house? What advantages or disadvantages would Chimay draw from having Soleilmont in its filiation today, tomorrow and a century from now? With Mr. Brohée we have weighed all the aspects of these two questions. You know Mr. Brohée's devotedness to your well-being. You can be assured that in the answers to these questions I myself do not seek anything but what is best. But I, unlike Mr. Brohée, cannot be satisfied with weighing only the advantages for Soleilmont; I have to consider the life at Chimay, independently of all personal sentiments of affection. It has been decided amongst us that I will give my opinion after consulting the Reverend Abbot General and Dom Norbert. That will take place immediately after Easter. I recommend this decision to your prayers, and to the prayers of the community. You must have an idea of how much all this preoccupies me.

And in July:

My Reverend Mother, at the next General Chapter, they will look after you. I have told the Bishop what I think. He told me

> what he intends to do. It is up to the Chapter to decide. I am very happy to be the reason for postponing the question of your definitive and complete affiliation. But Paternity is a serious matter that one must not assume without being sure that one can accomplish all the duties it involves. In the meantime, Yours, no matter what solutions the General Chapter may decide upon.

In December, it was decided: the Abbot of Westmalle would be the Father Immediate of Soleilmont. Dom Anselme wrote to Dom Alexis Presse: "The poor girls! They wept without shame before me because they were not auctioned off to Scourmont. And in fact, what an aberration it is that they were auctioned to Westmalle: what is this Flemish chaplain doing in a completely Wallon region? All right, leave it as it is."

Dom Anselme, however, did not try to hide from this trial of his Soleilmont sisters. He wrote them a cordial letter, full of nuances:

> Reverend Mother, I congratulate you, and I congratulate your community on the favorable outcome of your aggregation to the Order of Cistercians of the Strict Observance. With you, I rejoice in your happiness. You have already been Cistercians in reality for a number of years; you have had all the merits of nuns of this Order; but official juridical affiliation and affiliation to a house of monks remained an advantage you greatly desired. Now you have your stability in the Order of Cîteaux. You come back home for good after an absence of a hundred years—or almost—from the Order. You come back to the tradition of your family of Soleilmont, which already counts six centuries of Cistercian life. You begin your seventh century. You are certainly venerable! But especially, how happy you are! I congratulate you on your happiness. As for me, I still have some remorse about this matter: remorse about having been the cause of the delay of your definitive affiliation, because of my hesitations. Please forgive me. But still, and even more, I have a sort of sadness: the sadness of someone who would have wanted to will something and did not will it; who would have liked to devote himself to your family and who did not will to do so. Not that we were necessary to each other:

> Soleilmont did not need me. On the contrary, Soleilmont will receive more from another Father. But Soleilmont, because of its ancient tradition, and for so many reasons today, is so congenial to me that I consider it legitimate to love it and I would personally have loved to have a relationship with it—a family relationship—, more intimate than that of belonging to a same Order. But I alone am responsible for this sadness. It will in no way diminish your good. My wish is that your community will find renewed prosperity in its official affiliation. When I say "I wish," I say less than what I think. I think, I am persuaded that your community will become a numerous and excellent Cistercian community. With this assurance, My Reverend Mother, please accept for yourself and for your community my wishes for a long and perfect Cistercian life, and also, please believe in the attachment and the warm cordiality of your neighbor, the Abbot of Chimay.

But we know how tenacious women are. The Prioress of Soleilmont accepted her Flemish chaplain—all right. That did not mean that the Father Abbot of Scourmont, who lived just a few kilometres away and was free to go out, could not make a little innocent detour regularly to his Cistercian sisters. As far as he was concerned, Dom Anselme was prudent:

> Reverend Mother, . . . as for coming to Soleilmont in person, I had the intention to do so. I thought of going there toward the end of the year, even though I had decided not to accept the paternity. I knew that even after my refusal you would continue to offer me your generous hospitality; and for my part, I desired Soleilmont as a good place for me to make my annual retreat. Then, when I was about to carry out my project someone pointed out to me that doing so could appear to be tactless with regard to Westmalle. So I abstained from going to Soleilmont, not because I refused to go to see you, but because of another person. So let us wait for another occasion.

The Mother Prioress was crafty. So that Dom Anselme would not lose his interest in Soleilmont she invented reasons, both diversified and persistent, to call upon him. First of all she sent him a list of prayers, Masses and Communions that her sisters offered for him. The Father Abbot sent her the following sober reply:

> My Reverend Mother, how nice you are, and how delicate! Thank you for your pious attention: I thank your good community for the prayers that the sisters want to offer for me. You can be sure that I continue to have great affection for Soleilmont; and even, I dare say, solicitude.

Seeing that prayers did not have much effect on him, the Mother Prioress turned to a strategy of attack: Scourmont is neglecting us by not paying the bills we sent! She obtained excuses from Dom Anselme, who sent her some of Chimay's products:

> My Reverend Mother, I am very embarrassed that I failed you by not seeing to the payment of an invoice. I believed that the matter had been taken care of, because here the cellarer and secretary look after everything which concerns invoices to be paid and merchandise received. It suffices for them to be aware of what happened. You could have quite simply sent the invoice, at least, at the end of the month. I am correcting my wrongdoing as of today and am paying the overdue interest. Please accept a small package of our products. They are hardly anything. We do not have the wealth and generosity of heart that your most Reverend Father Immediate has, but all the same, if I can be of service to you I will not fail to do so, be it spiritual or temporal. It is a way of soothing my regret for not being all yours. I do not yet dare to go to Soleilmont. Excuse me; I have no doubts about your generous hospitality.

The Prioress felt that exchanging their products as gifts was a good approach. She sent Scourmont crates of apples from Soleilmont's orchards. Dom Anselme played the prioress' game, with great finesse:

> My Reverend Mother, it is you who are nice, I mean very nice; one could not be nicer. The apples arrived, all of them, in good condition. What good apples! The soil of Soleilmont has a

special quality which gives its fruits an aroma, a taste, and a flavour which are unequalled. For centuries it has been monastic soil: the fruits have that flavour. They are "civilized" fruits. Ours are still savage fruits, because they come from savage soil. There is, in fact, a great difference between the fruit—the same varieties—of Soleilmont and that of Scourmont. Two "mountains," but one is the mountain of the sun and the other the mountain of help—help that one needs. One recognizes the tree by its fruit. Your tree is very good. Your community is excellent. I thank you for the good things you have sent. The community will taste Soleilmont's fruits at noontime today. The monks will thank you when they recognize by their taste where they have come from; they will love Soleilmont for having such good nuns. Besides, believe me, here we all like you a lot. We often think of Soleilmont, the venerable Abbey of Soleilmont. In the chapter room, the coat of arms and the name of Soleilmont figure along with those of ancient abbeys such as Villers and La Cambre. Then why do you not come to Soleilmont, you will say?

Why am I not nice, as you say? It is because we are too little, too rustic to rise as high as you. We are the wild boars of the Ardennes. We have to stay in the forest. Perhaps one day? . . . The time will perhaps come, the time will probably come when it will be said and recognized that the abbey of Chimay was wrong in not accepting the paternity of Soleilmont. I am waiting for that. Still, do not think too much about the paternity of Scourmont as though it would be Soleilmont's golden age. Particularly, I am persuaded that I would not succeed in satisfying you as far as visits and sojourns at Soleilmont are concerned. You are better off now. One thing is sure: I remain very attached to Soleilmont. This attachment comes from veneration for your venerable abbey; fellow-feeling for your present community and from your way of understanding the Rule. I want to express this attachment by my devotedness. Yours,

Once again, and as a last try, the Mother Prioress was going to play her last feminine card: We live poorly. That would not have been the case if we had been assigned to Scourmont. This time Dom Anselme "snapped":

> My Reverend Mother, I am very happy that you are acting and conducting yourself with great simplicity with regard to us. It is the best token that you can give of the attachment of your house to ours. We are going to reply with the same simplicity and cordiality. We will always do everything that we possibly can to come to your assistance. So ask, and let us know your needs. This time, I propose the following arrangement. We will send you a cow which still gives 12 litres of milk a day, and is still capable of giving milk for several months: 4 or 5. You will feed her; you will have the milk; if she has a calf, you will sell it and keep what you are paid for it. But the cow will remain ours. If she dies, she dies as ours, without you having anything to pay. If you sell her, she will be sold for us. This way you have all the advantages of a milk cow in your barn. If she doesn't satisfy you, we can replace her: our cow will be a boarder with you. Very nice, isn't it? Say the word and we will send you the cow. What station? Yours, as always.

We might think that, after having exhausted all means of temptation, as the holy evangelist said, the Mother Prioress would leave things alone for a while. Think again! She still had two extra strings on her violin.

The first: even though he wasn't the Father Immediate, what would keep Dom Anselme from coming to preach the retreat to the community of Soleilmont? Here, the Father Abbot was trapped. How was he going to escape from this?

> Preach the retreat in 1927? There is still time to see about that. . . . In any case, it could be someone from Scourmont; for example, Father Prior. When you will have heard him, you will not want anyone else but him, and will always want him, and you will be right, and I will approve. Moreover, my cordiality and my devotion toward you remain assured.
>
> You have of course heard that I preach retreats to religious. And it is sometimes proper for me to accept. I acknowledge that I have received a request from the Trappistines of Maubec. But I do not feel that I have an aptitude for preaching to nuns. I am thinking about sending my Prior, who excels in such a setting. So I think that I could send you my Prior. So what are

> you complaining about? It is perfect. I do not see how, in that solution, I lack devotion toward you.
>
> Besides, you have an election coming up. And before heads of women whose bonnets are so easily on crooked, the one preaching never knows how his words will be interpreted. So leave this retreat until later.

The second violin string that the Mother Prioress made vibrate in Dom Anselme's ear was his solicitude for the Trappistines of Chimay. In 1920 these sisters had left their miserable refuge at Fourbechies and moved to a rather large tract of property near the edge of the town of Chimay, several kilometres from their brothers, the Trappists of Scourmont. When they arrived, they found nothing but a modest house which was very inadequate for the regular life of a numerous community. But having been used to what was worse than that, they valiantly squeezed in and settled there. Dom Anselme took over directing the work, because he liked to build. He sensed the jealousy of the Mother Prioress of Soleilmont, and courageously explained:

> Reverend Mother, one day soon I have to go to Lodelinsart, in your vicinity, to chant a pontifical Mass. Know that I will once again be so cruel as not to come to see you. It is painful and mean. There are so many mean things in life. And we need so much to be above all this politeness! We can serve God everywhere; there is good and evil everywhere. So, for me, who am the patron of the Cistercian community of Chimay, Soleilmont surpasses it in my esteem. But this esteem does not prevent my devotedness being directed by priority to the nuns of Chimay who wish to make a real foundation. Moreover, know that for the time being I am taking more interest in bricks than in the sisters, particularly for the construction of their church: it will have the same dimensions as Soleilmont's, but it will not have the same fragrance as yours. I give you my peace. Give me your confidence.

25

Caldey: A daughter worthy of her mother?

From about the year 1925 on, Scourmont numbered 102 religious. Very naturally, therefore, Dom Anselme began to think about making a foundation. For a while he was looking toward Spain, then envisioned a foundation in India. Did he speak here and there about his ideas? In any case, when one goes through his correspondence from 1925–1927 on, one finds letters from monks from just about everywhere telling him that they were interested in his project and ready to make a try of such a daring adventure under the patronage of Scourmont.

But then we see what happened! In the same way that he had sacrificed himself for the good of the Order by accepting to make the regular visitation in Congo, Dom Le Bail was going to put aside his personal projects in order to give preference once again to interests of the Cistercian family, and in this case those of the Roman Catholic Church. He was going to accept—it would be better to say generously offer—to take over Caldey Abbey, located in southwest Wales on Carmarthen Bay, two kilometres from the continent, and four kilometres from Tenby, the port and closest town. Today many people do not know that this Abbey, occupied by Anglican Benedictine monks, became well-known in 1913 because of the community's complete and unanimous change over to Roman Catholicism. From a historical point of view, it was a return to its right. The island of Caldey was peopled by monks from 450 until 1550, that is to say, from the origin of Christian life among the Celts of Great Britain until the Anglican Reform and the destruction of all Catholic institutions in England. After the Anglican monastic community became Roman Catholic, the Anglican Church cut off its subsidies to the Abbey which had become papist and prepared to acquire the island in retaliation for its defeat, as a sign of the bankruptcy of the monks who had abandoned it. It was at this moment that Pope Pius XI expressly asked the Order of Cîteaux to send Trappists to take back Caldey. The Holy See's proposition came to the attention of the General Chapter and, as Dom Anselme reported, "I dared to offer Scourmont's help. And I had no competitors in this matter."

In fact, it was not so simple as that, because it seems that the Order had first fixed its choice on the Abbot of Timadeuc, who absolutely did not want to impose this responsibility on his community. By discretion Dom Anselme did not admit that by his proposal he was coming to the aid of the poor abbot, who afterwards remained faithfully grateful to the Abbot of Scourmont. This explains Dom Anselme's letter to the Abbot of Timadeuc, dated March 28, 1928, after they both had visited Caldey:

> Reverend Father, I was delighted with the way this matter was thought out, examined and judged. During the six hours that the session lasted there were perfect understanding and freedom, good sentiments and tranquillity. On the whole, we would be happy to help out. But the matter does not look so easy. I took votes on four questions—and the result of the total vote was 22 against 6. I myself did not vote. So we have the opinion of our conventual chapter. What pleasant memories I have of our journey and your company. It was delightful from every point of view, at every moment and in every place. I told all that to the community, including our resolute and companionable walks, from morning until eight o'clock in the evening, with the aroma of cigarettes—and English cigarettes—, which did not "smoke me up." They found that detail very interesting. Here we are frank, you know. Your reputation as a man who is a man gained a lot from that. The reason is that here they are a bit tempted to believe that at Timadeuc there are only angels. It's beautiful, they say. But it is not like that in our monastery.

> We are men and, when all is said and done, poor men. But in fact, truthfully, these men who pretend to be angels, are they so sure that they will not fall to who knows where, as Pascal said? So the trip was lovely. It was even a pilgrimage for me, Breton that I am. . . . If there is no follow-up to the project, we will at least have had that. For this blessing, which you as well as the Most Reverend Father General have assured me of, that of the fraternity you showed me, I thank you.

The reaction from Timadeuc was not long in coming; it arrived on April 19. In the absence of the Father Abbot it was signed by the Prior, who had been to Caldey with his Abbot and Dom Anselme. By the tone of this letter we discover that Dom Anselme knew how to awaken simple and warm friendships.

> Dear Father Abbot Dom Anselme, our Father Abbot asks to be excused for being so late in answering your nice letter of March 28, but you no doubt know that we are on retreat. I am so happy to learn that everything has been settled in your conventual chapter, and to your best interests. It is certain that our Most Reverend Father has hands which are as generous as his heart—like yours, I might add—and I am happy about that because we, monks of Timadeuc, are among those who benefit from your magnanimity. I have only to wish you much success in what you have undertaken. It cannot fail, with religious like those of Scourmont: intelligent, regular, good workers. I would have been happy to accompany you again to this land of plenty where the shellfish are so fat and the cigarettes are so awful! But I ought to be here when my Abbot returns from America. Why don't you invite me to your community's official taking possession of the island? At the same time I would be glad to go and say goodbye definitively to Caldey. Dear Father Abbot, I believe that there is no reason to worry about this foundation which is being made in such advantageous conditions. The beginning will be a little difficult; of course, but you can send a serious and numerous contingent from Chimay; if vocations arrive after a few years, your daughter will be very prosperous; and that will be God's blessing on your devotedness to the Order and to the Church. Sincerely and with affection devotedly yours.

That Dom Anselme wanted to send only monks of value to Caldey is confirmed by an extant letter he wrote during this same month of April, 1928, to his friend Dom Alexis Presse:

> I never send anywhere any monk of mine who might be only half-religious. I will not send any doubtful subjects to Caldey. I am, however, sending them a monk who is ill, Father Odilon: but that is a grace that I am offering them.

After formally inaugurating the foundation in January, Dom Anselme learned several months later that some questions concerning individual monks were suddenly and too rapidly disturbing the cloudless sky of the foundation. He immediately realized the risks and, on May 29, 1929, on the occasion of the opening of the novitiate, he spoke out in clear and perspicacious terms:

> It is the daughter of Chimay, this posterity. Caldey should keep the spirit of Chimay, like a daughter ought to perpetuate her mother. . . . Consequently, so that they may imbibe this spirit it is fitting that Caldey's recruits from overseas should not only have the example and teaching of the seniors, but should see and have contact with the novitiate of Chimay. For this reason we are not hesitating to send Chimay's novice master himself for this work, and with him the most cherished and esteemed young men of our novitiate. . . . No doubt, places and material are willingly being prepared to receive them; it is even easy to prepare one's heart for joy and cordial hospitality. It is more difficult and more important, however, to prepare the moral setting where these novices can be formed without scandal, develop without obstacles, and themselves become a favorable milieu for attracting and keeping recruits from Great Britain. You know that a community has the novitiate that it merits by its own conduct. So the duty of the seniors is to organize their life so as to merit a numerous and choice posterity. First of all, in this duty of preparing the path for the novices whom God and Chimay send you, it seems to me that there is reason to beg you to do away with all exterior and interior defiance, criticism and murmuring concerning the success of your work,

> and the way things are going for you. If you are continually saying openly that there is nothing to hope for, there is nothing that can be done; if one thinks that everything is bad—except oneself, of course—, if you are waiting for everything around you to be perfect before doing something yourself, it is evident that you should not wish for others to come after you to share this wretchedness, and we would be doing something cruel if we sent there these dear young people who are happy at Chimay. Not that this silent patience—*tacita conscientia*—means to be blindly optimistic. In this foundation it is impossible not to see the immensity of the work and the lack of means. The divergence between the means and the end may even appear to increase as efforts are being made. But among the founders, there is God. In monastic history, in the history of Chimay just as in that of thousands of foundations, you know that this founder has accomplished great things with what was thought to be foolish and stupid. It is even his law to choose what is weak to confound the strong. . . . A balanced judgment, in face of the difficulties and shortcomings of a foundation, refrains from recriminations and murmuring. All that sort of thing can do nothing but discourage others and at the same time increase the bitterness in one's own soul.

It seems that the message was not clearly understood, or that the Superior perhaps did not know how to deal with tensions, which are inherent in any community. From 1929 until 1934, Dom Anselme wrote continually to him in order to encourage and pacify him, to make him smile and free him.

> As concerns the rumors which are going around, never torment yourself thoroughly. You are allowed to be troubled for a quarter of an hour. Then silence. After such commotion it often seems that everything is falling apart. And yet, everything continues to go on.
>
> A superior should be magnanimous: he should not be weighed down for more than a quarter of an hour, at least during the day when he is awake. As for the night, that is something else: you do not sleep; you learn to sleep habitually only four hours.

> Be courageous when you are faced with difficulties. The difficulty for a Superior is to support human misery with a calm heart. To want everything and everyone to be perfect is to wish for something impossible. The Superior is put there to be continually in apprehension and anguish. If in the evening you go to sleep without cares and troubles, it is the sign of a bad day. What is more, when you feel elated because you have succeeded in something, you can conclude that things are going very badly.
>
> Try to insist on unity. I am tired of doing that. Because everywhere, in every human society, there is a storm every day which tends toward disunion. Between Chimay and Caldey, I realize that Caldey makes me suffer and fear more, by its lack of unity. Caldey is still too much "me," for me not to be sensitive to everything which concerns it. Because of that I feel bad, as though the trouble came about because of my fault. Goodbye for the time being, son! Remain in peace: I am the one who will bear the weight of the visit.

It seems that one reason for the difficulties Caldey was experiencing was the way several subalterns of the monastery were imposing their authority and disciplinary demands. Dom Anselme, who did everything possible at Chimay to create a climate of responsibility and freedom, was particularly grieved and vexed:

> Reverend Father Dom Godefroid has just left us to become auxiliary Superior at Cîteaux. In this circumstance, I reminded all those in positions of responsibility and all the members of the community that men pass but the monastic Church continues. Men are the instruments of divine action only for a period of time. No man owns a rank or responsibility for souls. God and his Christ alone are possessors of souls, and souls should be possessed only by God. I wish you, at Caldey, to have the sentiments which at this time hearten your Mother-house. In spite of its sorrow, it is in admirable peace and confidence.
>
> You spoke to me about a brother who is sick with anemia: don't say that it is because of the sea. I have learned that, at Cîteaux, since the arrival of Dom Godefroid everyone is fine

and the sick have rejoined the ranks. But at Caldey the monks feel nothing but restrictions and constraint: don't speak, don't go out, don't have butter, don't, don't. . . . Your two assistants are night caps, wet blankets. They swear by nothing but the Usages and holiness. You see what the results of that are. Of course freedom, being at ease, fraternal gests, conversations can have disadvantages. But when a person feels that he is being treated as a free and reasonable man, he takes upon himself to remain within the limits. You would do well to give a few instructions on freedom of the soul, sociableness, appropriate openness and mutual confidence. You can have your two assistants read this letter. They can condemn our way, my way, Dom Godefroid's and that of the novitiate here. But then, don't complain about your failures.

It seems that in spite of these difficulties, the community was capable of growing and even showed signs of hope, because on January 6, 1934, the foundation of Caldey was raised to the status of an autonomous Priory. Fr. Lefèvre, forty-two years old, was elected the first titular Prior. The mandate for the foundation, announced publicly by Dom Anselme, related the history of the project and revealed his enthusiasm, which had not changed.

Brother Anselme Le Bail, Abbot of Notre Dame de Scourmont, of the Order of Cistercians of the Strict Observance, to all the religious of his abbey, monks and lay brothers, zeal for the extension of the Reign of Christ.

Following our request, after approval by the General Chapter of our Order the Holy See deigned to raise our foundation of Notre Dame of Caldey to the dignity of a Priory and to establish it as an autonomous house "*sui iuris.*" The community of Notre Dame of Scourmont announces with joyful welcome the birth of its first daughter, Notre Dame of Caldey.

The most lofty expression of this joy should be thanksgiving to the Most Holy Trinity. It has pleased the Father to let us participate in his power of being the principle of all life and all good. We become co-adjutors of Our Lord Jesus Christ in the expansion of his Church. And the Holy Spirit truly seems to inspire us, since we have been able to establish a school of charity in another country. We wanted to accomplish a work of God when we founded Caldey. Now that this has been achieved it is not imprudent to state that this foundation is, in fact, his work. So let us also give thanks and glory to the Father, Son and Holy Spirit. Three conventual Masses will be celebrated for this intention on the feast of the Epiphany: the morning Mass, the Mass *de Beata*, and the principal Mass; they will be the most adequate expression of our thanksgiving. Nevertheless, to help us to grasp it better, and to make this thanksgiving rise up from the hearts of all of us by a personal and spontaneous act, we take pleasure in recalling the intentions which inspired us in founding Notre Dame of Caldey.

We thought, and we judge, that a community of contemplative monks does not fully attain its goal if it does not have the apostolic zeal which goes so far as the will and effort to bring about, according to its means and form of life, the expansion of the Reign of Our Lord Jesus Christ. Life is motion. The Christian life is a social life where each member, each constituent part, should work toward achieving the perfection of the whole body, of the whole Church, without which one could not attain one's own individual perfection.

Personal holiness, like charity, is of course expansive by nature, and in itself reflects on the whole Church. Thus, without any special intention or exterior action, the monk who grows in personal holiness acquires apostolic zeal. In practice, the ordinary monk—because this is common to human nature—needs some motivating objective in order to intensify his personal charity. He risks falling asleep and not to live fully, the monk who has no care about giving himself. Expansion in depth by intensity of prayer, and by assimilation of spiritual teaching, is the ordinary type of monastic action.

As for the community, motion is more explicitly a sign of life. More perceptible, more exterior because it is a society, the community needs to feel that it is accomplishing works that are profitable to the expansion of Christ's reign. It is not a question—this you know well enough—of ministry to souls. Monastic discipline ought to be maintained in its purity. But when God blesses a community like ours by multiplying the number of its members to the point that it has increased from sixty-five members to one hundred and five in a few years, is this not a sign that God expects it to make a foundation in order to bring to another country the blessings of the monastic life? That is what we have thought, and it is the reason why we have wanted to make a foundation.

When this project came into view, it would have been legitimate and glorious to want to bring back to life an ancient abbey in our own country. It seemed to us, however, that it would be more in conformity with the present outlook of the Church to implant the monastic life, in its Cistercian form, in new countries, or rather, in countries which have been deprived of their heritage to this type of life. Is doing missionary work in our own way not more advantageous for the propagation of the Church? A particular Church, a regional Church, is not perfect if it does not give rise to an indigenous clergy in addition to the faithful, and if it does not offer various practices of the religious life to souls of good will. More particularly, monasteries of contemplative life crown the building up of Church.

In conformity with this outlook, we thought of making a foundation in India or Madagascar. We also thought about Sudan, or all the African countries above the regions of the Bantu; these places, excluded for the time being, seem worthy of attention and to offer possibilities for the contemplative life. Every foundation is possible and desirable, wherever humanism is developed and there are enough Christians.

In the meantime, revival of Caldey, in Wales, was imposed on the Order by the Holy See, and accepted by the 1927 General Chapter. During that same Chapter we dared to offer the devotedness of the community of Notre-Dame de Scourmont to furnish the new community which would occupy Caldey in the name of and under the Rule of the Order. We have not had any competitors in this request.

The foundation replied—and how fully!—to all our preceding aspirations. Going to Caldey, in Wales, meant going on mission; it meant establishing the Cistercian life in a country which because of the departure of the Benedictines was completely lacking in monasteries for men. The Anglican country of the British Isles, with the exception of Ireland, presented all the needs and difficulties implied in the establishment of the contemplative life in a place where the regional Church had to be restored. But of all the parts of the British Isles, Wales was and remains the most needy, and the most obstinate in lack of faith in the Catholic Church. Our goals, the goals of our community in founding Caldey, are therefore first of all an apostolic goal: that is to say, to make present and visible in a non-Catholic country the practice of the Catholic life, in a form respected as a sign of its holiness and its catholicity; then, to work by monastic means alone for the conversion or reunion of the Welsh people and Anglicans to the Catholic Church; finally, but lastly, offer a possibility for native Cistercian recruitment, so that the Church in west Britain may also have its crown of contemplative life.

We pray our religious of Forges and Caldey, we pray our successors and descendants to preserve faithfully the remembrance of these intentions and to observe them with the same significance and in the same order. Tomorrow as today, they should guide the dedication of both communities. Caldey becomes autonomous in its government. But all the same, Caldey remains effectively a work of Notre-Dame de Scourmont. These goals should be maintained by the Motherhouse in every way possible. If children sometimes seem to be forgetful of their parents, can a mother forget her child?

For what has been already accomplished with respect to these goals, let us thank God. Again, for the past, it is fitting for us to give thanks for the temporal blessings which God has granted so abundantly, in an extraordinary way, to our foundation at Caldey. Thanks to God, thanks to our benefactors, the expenses of the foundation have been steadily covered without inconvenience to the Motherhouse. And thanks to the labor of the founders, after only two years of existence the daughterhouse has not needed one cent from the founding house.

And now We, Abbot, we want to express our gratitude to the entire community of Notre-Dame de Scourmont. After God, the community of Scourmont is the real founder of Caldey, the creator of Caldey. No individual can pride himself by claiming it is his. Caldey is the work of a community: the community wanted it; the community gave of itself to it; the community gave it all its interest. Of course, the initiative to maintain Caldey in the Roman Catholic Church and perpetuate a monastery there was due to the Most Reverend Father Dom Ollitrault, Abbot General of the Order at that time. Let us express our thanks to him. But the whole burden of this monastic accomplishment was assumed by the community of Notre-Dame de Scourmont. To it, our gratitude; and, in compensation, the assurance of its personal prosperity.

Among all the members of this community, We, the Abbot, want to signal out in order to thank them more particularly the founders of Caldey. They are members of Scourmont who have given themselves for life, insofar as it depends on them. Religious life is already a donation. They have given themselves twice, adding to their dedication to monastic works the renunciation of their country, their native tongue, relationships and customs, and the very special gift of themselves to the labor which a small community implies. But they are aware of our gratitude. And what is more, Christ has already rewarded them with joy.

We would like to thank with a very particular nuance and with compassionate tenderness several of the founders, those who, we might say, fell under the painful burden. They will understand. With them, we can say: we have suffered; we have remained silent. It is not appropriate to make a display of one's troubles. But they know that at no moment, at no minute, have We, their Father Abbot, ceased to respect them, love them and be grateful to them.

Finally, the great adventure, predicted as being dismal and presumptuous in 1928, has reached its accomplishment. To our daughter, today the only mistress of her ship, after God: a prosperous voyage for many centuries. Or again, let us greet her with the monastic wish that we address to a monk who has just been received into the community: "*Dominus custodiat introitum suum et exitum suum.*"

And this present mandate will be preserved in the archives and transcribed in entirety in the book of *Annals*.

Given at Notre-Dame de Scourmont, on the Epiphany of the year of grace 1934, the fifth anniversary of the exordium of Caldey.

During the years of the Second World War, the Father Abbot was, of course, unable to visit Caldey. That did not prevent him from continuing to have great solicitude for his dear daughter. In 1942, he wrote:

> My very dear children, what is most important is to preserve the life of the family, even with exceptions to the customs of our life. But to stay together as a family is the best guarantee for the future. Here, too, our preoccupation is to maintain the family. Up until now we are succeeding, in spite of the difficulties which are as big as yours: sometimes we are obliged to go a long way for the work that is necessary for keeping up our life. But what is important is that we are staying together. I ask you all, and each one, to hold good.

After the war Caldey still gave him quite a few worries which, in addition to his other preoccupations, finished by wearing him out. In February, 1949, while he was visiting the Island, the monks noticed that he did not go outside much, unlike his usual habit. Had he already experienced some sort of presentiment of a catastrophe? Before leaving for the Continent, he said to the Prior, Dom Albert Derzelle, in a more or less serious way: "Especially, don't go out of your way to come to my funeral!" A month later he was struck down by an attack of cerebral congestion which made it impossible for him to accomplish his duties as abbot.

26

From Fourbechies to Chimay: Notre Dame de la Paix

After living for years at Fourbechies, in 1919 the Cistercian nuns of Saint-Paul-aux-Bois decided to move to Chimay, *"in pago Chimacensi"*—as the archives from that time say—and to found what would later become Notre Dame de la Paix Abbey. After their expulsion from France resulting from the Combes Laws, these Cistercian nuns, originally from Gomerfontaine in the diocese of Rouen-Beauvais, had taken refuge in a miserable shelter where they suffered from hunger, cold and lack of hygiene.

The Abbot of Scourmont, being at a distance of several kilometres from Chimay, was inevitably indicated to help these nuns pull through the moral and material trial of this exodus. Dom Anselme would be infinitely discreet in helping them, but also energetic, and he would use the virile authority they needed. Fortunately, six letters addressed to Fourbechies, dating between March 25 and July 20, 1919, have been preserved. The lengthy quotations from these letters given here will show us Dom Anselme's paternal solicitude toward his "very dear daughters" and toward the new Prioress whom he called *"Filia carissima."*

At the time her community was moving, the Mother Prioress profited from the occasion to put aside the burden of her function. Consequently, along with all their emotions resulting from changing their place to live, her sisters had to assume another change: the election of a new prioress. Things went satisfactorily, and Dom Anselme congratulated them:

> My dear daughters, I am persuaded that your community is continuing to live in the peace and unity that it has always enjoyed. You want this because of your love for Our Lord Jesus Christ, and for the good of your family. You should also give Reverend Mother Adelaide, your former Prioress and such a meritorious Mother, this witness of your attachment to her as a person. If, in fact, you want to give her a real sign of your attachment, you should continue to observe what she has always taught you: charity, which unites the religious to their Superior, and the religious among themselves. This will also be your best preparation to receive your new Prioress. Your new Prioress, Reverend Mother Madeleine, has given her consent, with the apprehension that is understandable in the face of her new responsibility. Furthermore, she could not wisely have refused it, considering the will of the majority of you, and faced with the way I asked her. She said to me: "I always reply *Fiat* to whatever is asked of me." So all I had to do was to explain everything to her and wait for her consent, which she could not refuse to God and to you.
>
> Let a song rise from your hearts in spite of the legitimate sadness which may tighten them, because above the pain of the present moment you must see God's action at work in persons and communities. I pray that this renewal in the government—the change of the person in charge of the community—and the change of the location of the monastery which will soon take place may be occasions for the renewal of souls. For that to come about, it is of absolute importance for you to preserve, interiorly and exteriorly, calmness and recollection among yourselves (March 25, 1919).

Several days later, it was to his *"Filia carissima"* that Dom Anselme wrote, first of all to organize the liturgy—as he liked to do—for the installation of the new Prioress. It was a question of some courageous acts which were necessary:

> My very dear daughter, by now your soul must once again be serene. And Our Lord must have strongly impressed in your mind your mission to be his minister for the sanctification of your religious, your daughters. It is a ministry which of course does not include all the powers of a priest, but which according

> to Saint Benedict consists, for an abbot or a prioress, in being a "vicar of Christ." Accept this invitation with great simplicity, but worthily occupy the place of Christ in your monastery.
>
> And now, let's get down to work! Your installation will take place on Saturday, April 5, with Saint Julienne of Mount Cornillon as your patroness. Since you will arrive at Chimay only the evening before, you do not need to be present at any community exercises. Father Charles will introduce you; and you will occupy the prioress' room. All the same, if you desire to attend the Office, you should take the place of the Sub-Prioress, leaving the Prioress' stall vacant.
>
> There will be one single ceremony for your installation and the simple profession of the novices. After the Gospel I will proceed to your installation behind the grill; then your acceptance and the transmission of the keys. Your sisters will make their promise of obedience. Then I will receive the profession vows of the novices, and the whole ceremony will end with the Te Deum.

Several days before the ceremony, Dom Anselme wrote to the Mother Prioress that he had been thinking about the menu for the sisters. Here once again we find the convivial style of the Father Abbot and his freedom of spirit:

> I would like to enhance the day's menu by something extra: a little glass of wine and a cake. You can hold me responsible for that. I will furnish the wine. The Reverend Mother Abbess of Soleilmont could perhaps furnish some waffle cakes, like those I ate at Soleilmont—they were so good! Fifty, or let's say, a hundred. It is hardly anything, but that seems good to me. Dear daughter, the time for thorns will come fast enough. Prepare your hearts for hard work: when that time comes, you will have to be a strong woman. Accept my blessing.

But the Father Abbot's solicitude with regard to the new Prioress did not stop there. He advised her not to speak to the community on the day of her installation. The following Sunday, however, "it is fitting that you should give them an instruction which goes with this occasion," he told her. Very ingeniously, Dom Anselme suggested the theme for her talk, pointing out even more ingeniously that it was on that subject that he had spoken to his community when he came back from the 1914–1918 war. "It is only my opinion," he said, "and I leave you full liberty as to what you will say." "In your place, here is what I would say":

> When the Father Immediate told me that I was elected, he said that in this circumstance your choice was the expression of God's will. It is in this spirit of conformity to God's will that I have accepted the office of Prioress. Serve our Lord Jesus Christ by being completely yours: that is what I want. May our Lord and his holy Mother grant that I may accomplish this.

Anxious about how the change of Prioress would go, Dom Anselme suggested to Mother Madeleine that she should speak quite a lot about Mother Adelaide:

> My wish is that I may realize this ideal following the example of Reverend Mother Adelaide. For me just as for you, she is a mother, our Mother Prioress. As witness of my personal inclinations, and also to show the esteem and gratitude that we owe her for her thirty-three years—so worthy and fruitful—as Prioress, and finally to keep in mind that it is only her refusal to prolong her time in office which has led you to elect me unanimously, with the consent of the Father Immediate I give her the title of Prioress of Honor, whose place will be first after your present Prioress. Look upon this as a sign that I want to maintain the tradition among you, and to preserve in the government of our community what has always been done and loved.

Over and above that, Dom Anselme was not in favor of expressing compliments to the new Prioress. "You can take these suggestions simply as a guide!" he concluded; "You will be able to find the right note better than I, a note from the heart and a simple one" (March 29).

The second part of the letter is more prosaic:

> It will be necessary to deal with the Abbot General so that he will advance the funds for the purchase of the property—if he is too slow about it, Scourmont will advance the money; you will have to make an appointment with the notary at Chimay, Master Lemaur; the sisters who will be the purchasers will have to be present, driven there from the monastery and back home again in Scourmont's car.
>
> I feel sorry for you, my very dear daughter, that you have to begin your duties as Prioress with temporal work on a house! But the future of the Community depends on it. During this transfer your preoccupation should be to preserve calmness and recollection in your family. Besides, Father Charles will be there at all times to help you. And if you need a policeman or judge, I will be there. Lots of the changes will shock the old sisters. You can blame them on me: "The Father Immediate wants it, the Father Immediate is doing that." Put me there to plug the holes. That is my place in your community. Amen! (March 29).

In a letter dated May 22, the great day was just four days away:

> My very dear daughter, we are now going to go into action. The notary has been notified. The act will be drawn up and signed on May 26, at noon, the legal hour, in the office of Master Lemaur, on the road from Baileux to Chimay. You, along with your sisters and me, will be present at the reading of the act. I will pay the amount for the purchase in the name of the proprietors, who will afterwards owe this sum to the Abbot of Notre-Dame de Scourmont. In addition to this, you will sign the acknowledgement of the sum advanced. After the reading and signature of the act, and after having lunch at the Hospice of Chimay like our founding Fathers of Saint Joseph did, all together we will take possession of the new monastery of Chimay. You no doubt think that this taking possession will begin with a religious act, in order to put the place in the hands of its true proprietors, Christ Jesus and Our Lady. Your heart, so pious and delicate, has already thought of that. We will do it very simply, by reciting or chanting some prayers. The

> solemnity of the transfer and installation will come later on, at the right time.

Installing the new Prioress who was still at Fourbechies, and taking possession of the house at Chimay were nothing compared with organizing the moving of the community. It is an adventure that is not frequent even in our day. How much energy, practical sense and considerateness the Father Abbot gave proof of during this picturesque exodus! To relate all that in its slightest details is not useless, because it helps us to enter still further into the mind and heart of Dom Anselme, whom some people have a tendency to classify as an intellectualist. During this whole adventure, he showed that he was at the same time father, mother and brother.

At Soleilmont, where he made a stopover, he wrote a letter to Mother Madeleine on June 13. Having a good understanding of feminine sensitivity, without saying so explicitly, he suggested that the community of Chimay deserved to have the same comfort as the community of Soleilmont:

> My very dear daughter, everything that I see around me here, everything that I see at Soleilmont, makes me think of you by the contrast of conditions: here the regular places are beautiful and the outbuildings have been completed; at Chimay, everything remains to be done. I sympathize with your worries and I entrust you to God, the author and great lover of Peace. "*Deus pacis auctor et amator.*" Later, we will have to work out a theology of Peace: a beautiful question which I will study and teach you, and which you will put into practice.
>
> While I am here, I am studying the history of Soleilmont, which was begun in 1088 but was completed only in the fifteenth century. So you, founding Mother of Notre Dame de la Paix, you have five centuries ahead of you. Let us not be too quick therefore in saying: "Our work, ours." Let's be calm. Let's not rush!
>
> When I leave Soleilmont, before stopping by to see you I am going to Brussels to buy you some good and beautiful things. You see that my stay at Soleilmont is not estranging me from

> you, and that sharing my affection does not diminish it. When I will arrive at your monastery, the Reverend Father Abbot of Saint-Sixte will no doubt be there. It would be advisable for you to prepare a festive meal for him, to touch his heart and untie the strings of his purse. But I don't put too much hope in that. All the same, try to speak Flemish with him, won't you?!

In a letter dated May 29, on the feast of the Ascension, Dom Anselme courageously approached the subject of cleanliness:

> My very dear daughter, blessed Ascension Day: "*Ipsi quoque mente in coelestibus habitemus.*" To dwell in spirit already in our heavenly home is a wish that is appropriate for you and even more so for me, at this time when we are so occupied with things of this world. And all the more so, because in this letter I must attack the problem of vermin. *Primo*: major and radical excommunication of the race of all that stings or bites, by baths, washing clothes, and vigilant policing. *Secundo*: Make sure that the bedclothes are clean. If necessary, Scourmont will furnish you with new blankets in order to ward off what was pointed out in *primo*. *Tertio*: the personal clothing necessary for each religious must be in a state of perfect cleanliness. The Father Immediate will make a "customs inspection": brrr . . . ! *Quarto*: the straw mattress cases are to be washed before you move, and at Chimay they will be filled with straw furnished by Scourmont.

But how many other problems Dom Anselme had to think of, and for which he had foreseen solutions! What will the sisters eat during the first days after they will have moved in? Scourmont will bring them food each day. And even for the first year: "I have given an order at Scourmont to plant more vegetables than we need. You will receive what is left over. Don't worry about that." Curtains? Dom Anselme arranged that the sisters at Soleilmont would take care of them. Let the Chimay sisters go there and keep their eyes wide open. The sisters will need a watch dog: the Father Abbot has found a place to get one at Brussels.

The community Notre Dame de la Paix was very conscious of all the Father Immediate was doing for them. On July 26, Dom Anselme wrote:

> *Filia carissima*, when I arrived at Scourmont, the basket which you so carefully put in the car was opened, and I found in it the delicateness of all the kindness of your heart. Really, your generosity is inexhaustible, and your considerateness is unfailing. It is true that all these things should not surprise me, because I have read that a mother's heart is always able to guess needs and desires: you have this maternal quality. In the name of my community, I thank you. At noon tomorrow, in the refectory there will be an "extra" to celebrate the arrival of our venerated Father Abbot Dom Norbert.

We will conclude this delightful adventure of the transfer from Fourbechies to Chimay by several passages from the last letter of Dom Anselme, dated July 26. They give an astonishing portrait of Abbot Le Bail:

> This morning I meditated on your transfer from Fourbechies to Chimay. Must I go to Fourbechies before the transfer? If my presence—the presence of a torturer—is going to make the old sisters suffer, it is useless for me to come. It is useless to add to their sorrows by my presence, and I understand that very well. If it is suitable for me to come, what would I say? I would explain the sense of this transfer, from the sadness of leaving Saint-Paul-aux-Bois to the joy of founding a permanent House and a complete Monastery; and I would express my assurance that the Community will be able to develop and flourish in the perfect practice of the Benedictine Rule and our Cistercian Usages.
>
> You know as well as I do about the bits of gossip which say that I do not have a right idea of the monastic life and especially not of the life of nuns. As far as all that goes, I do not want to get caught up in the inconsistencies of feminine judgments. The point on which I am in agreement is that it is necessary to proceed gradually in order to reach a patient transformation of minds.

> So wouldn't the best solution be to delegate Dom Norbert for this transfer? For Fourbechies, he is the "Father" who has not been replaced. At Scourmont, I must admit in all simplicity that he has been replaced because here we like a way of acting that is frank, intellectual and military: that's my strong side. And my weak side is that the needs for suavity are less urgent.
>
> So Dom Norbert would do well—with his touch that is so delicate, establishing all your sisters in suavity and peace—to make the name of the new monastery a reality. With me, it would risk meriting the name of Our Lady "of war." So while Dom Norbert will be at the Chapter I will be busy with bricks. You see: we have to be complementary to each other. He will do you good by speaking to you. I will prove my affection by building for you. You will have me with you for a long time still. You will have Dom Norbert for only several days: profit from his presence. Dom Norbert is my friend, and yet I do not monopolize him at your expense. I offer him to you. See how much I love you.

With two nuns of Notre Dame de la Paix we have reminisced about Dom Le Bail. Among their remembrances, there were many anecdotes that we already knew quite well. What is astonishing is that these two elderly religious, seeking among their remembrances, both began to speak about him by saying: "Dom Anselme, he was charity personified. Dom Anselme, he was goodness itself."

27

The dismal crossroad of the Second War

For the community of Scourmont the Second World War was a greater trial than the First War. During the latter in fact, except for a dozen religious who were called up for active service, the monks could remain within the walls of the Abbey and lead their regular life there rather peacefully. It wasn't the same at all during the second war.

From September, 1939 on, Dom Anselme saw twenty-four of his sons leave, called up in the service of Belgium and France; others followed in May, 1940. With his personnel so drastically diminished, the Father Abbot stayed where he was. Even from a simply human point of view, it was wise not to leave the Abbey; it was courageous to resist the wave of general panic. And to the eyes of those who fled, the Father Abbot and his monks were lost men, doomed to being massacred by the enemy troops. What is more, a rumor went around that Dom Anselme was dead and that his monastery was completely destroyed.

Several years after the war Dom Anselme had the pleasure of learning about a funeral eulogy composed for him in Ireland in 1940 by Dom Celsus, Abbot of Mount Melleray. The rumor of his death had spread that far! Dom Celsus called Dom Anselme an "outstanding Abbot," an appreciation which heartily amused Father Anselme. He himself gave an interpretation of the expression: "Not a remarkable and extraordinary Abbot, no; but an Abbot apart, certainly not like the others, 'out,' outside what is normal, habitual or conventional."

In spite of Dom Anselme's tenacity, however, by June, 1940, the Abbey received an order from the military authorities to evacuate the monastery within several hours. A moving note written in the Father Abbot's handwriting is extant, describing this first departure in catastrophic circumstances:

> We have remained in the place of our stability and our monastic profession as long as it has been within our will and power to do so. We are abandoning our abbey only because of an order from an authority that is physically incontestable. We are leaving only insofar as this is imposed upon us, ready to come back as soon as possible.
>
> We, all of us, should remain a community, dependent on the established hierarchy, and in union of fraternal charity.
>
> We will take as personal baggage a chalice, the breviary (the four volumes, insofar as possible). Each one can add a blanket and even his cowl. If possible, this personal baggage will be transported on a cart. Besides that, we will provide what is basically necessary for what concerns food and clothing.
>
> The only moral guideline I give you is to keep respectable silence, without any demonstration, either by words or signs.
>
> *Benedicat vos Omnipotens et Misericors Deus, Pater, et Filius, et Spiritus Sanctus.*
>
> A description then follows of the condition of the sick of the Community. The infirm and sick who cannot move about: Br. Dieudonné, Clément, Arsène and Arnold. Those who cannot leave on foot : Fr. Sébastian, Samuel, Guerric, Joseph, Camille, Maurice, Remacle, Georges. Mesieurs. Cordonnier, Willain, Ceppens, and Madame Stockman.
>
> We want to have a cart for transporting the baggage.

This group of evacuated monks found a place of refuge at Vergnies, near Beaumont. They lived crammed in there for five weeks, lacking everything. But it was summer, and they risked going back to Scourmont where they found everything plundered and left in a state of repugnant filthiness by the troops who had gone through there.

The second evacuation took place in April, 1942. It was harder for the monks and more decisive, even if it was less sudden. The order to evacuate by April 12 reached the Father Abbot on April 1. He immediately obtained a place of temporary refuge in the château of Chimay, generously put at the disposition of the monks by the caretaker of the Prince. Dom Anselme informed the community of this as follows:

> To my brothers: The date for evacuation of the monastery of Notre-Dame de Scourmont has been fixed by the military authorities for April 12. We will celebrate the Holy Week Services and Easter in our abbatial Church. On Holy Thursday—*In Coena Domini*—, the conventual Mass will be sung at 8:30. All the brothers at the château should take care to fulfill their Pascal obligation in the church of their monastery. Father Cornelius will celebrate Mass at the château. Brother Ambrose and Brother Leopold will watch over things at the château and prepare what is necessary in the kitchen.
>
> At the Abbey, after *mixt*, (we will) return to the chateau for dinner and afternoon work. Good Friday and Holy Saturday, our brothers at the château should attend the Office of the Altar in the church of their monastery. Easter Sunday, Solemn Mass in the monastery as usual.

The Father Abbot's Holy Thursday homily after the Gospel has been preserved:

> My dear sons, today we celebrate our last Holy Thursday at Scourmont. It is very normal for us to draw a parallel between the Last Supper of Our Lord Jesus Christ which he celebrated with his apostles and the Last Supper that we are celebrating at Scourmont before our forced evacuation. There are certainly parallels which we could make: but let us be careful not to pretend to be martyrs for our religion, persecuted for our faith, or crucified. To do so would be to yield to easy eloquence and to a literary theme which does not coincide with reality. Let us respect the profound divergences which separate these two Suppers; let us speak the language of the Gospel: Yes, yes. No, no.
>
> Let us remember events that are still recent: On May 10, 1940, 43 out of the 84 religious in the community had to abandon the

cloister, scatter and expose themselves to death. On May 28, 1940, the community as such was forced to evacuate. In less than 24 hours all were obliged to leave everything, taking along on one single cart whatever was necessary for the life of the soul, mind and body. The community had to leave the monastery in the most complete uncertainty, not knowing where it would find food and shelter. And yet, although it seemed that this was the destruction of Scourmont, the monks all got together again and found their property intact. In March and April, 1942, we again found ourselves in the same critical situation: things were dispersed (which made for excellent practice in keeping an inventory, and permitted us to make a proper distinction among what was necessary, useful or superfluous, and even to recognize the trifles to which we had become attached by mania or by an instinct to possess). The places where the community assembled are the worst exposed. We have no idea what has happened to the buildings. As for me, I have no feelings of real sadness at the thought that these buildings might be destroyed, even though they are buildings I myself built.

The only sadness, the only anxiety which occupies all of us has as its object the very future of the ecclesial community of Scourmont. Will the community be able to preserve its unity? Will the ecclesial community of Scourmont survive this trial?

This is a question which causes us anguish, because our Church does not have a character that is absolute. It is not absolutely necessary to the universal Church; nor is it a necessity for our vocation, which can be lived in another setting; nor is it an absolute necessity for our eternal salvation, which could be worked out elsewhere.

Granting the elements of unlikeness between our last supper and the Last Supper, I recognize that we have the duty to maintain the community. Now, Christ's Last Supper and the discourse which followed the Supper form the best line of conduct for us to follow.

We should force ourselves to do what Christ did.

What was the communion which existed between Christ and his Apostles? It was the efficacious sign of unity in the primitive Church, reduced to the dimensions of the apostolic college. The Last Supper was the consecration of their unity and the last manifestation of the unity of the apostolic college and Christ, at the same time as it was the beginning of the true unity of the Church.

This sign of unity was necessary at the moment of the apparent annihilation of Christ's work on the eve of the dispersion of his flock.

In the discourse of the Last Supper Christ developed the same theme of unity: unity with the Father, unity of the apostles with Christ; unity of the Church and the whole of humanity throughout time and space.

What is the particular meaning of our communion at Scourmont's last supper? I said at the beginning: Our Church of Scourmont does not represent a character of absolute necessity for the universal Church, for our vocation or for our salvation.

Nevertheless, in our state of life, presupposing our monastic vocation, the Church of Scourmont is necessary for most of us in order to live our monastic vocation and attain salvation.

Consequently, my line of conduct as Abbot, faced with the withdrawal of a professed monk who has solemn vows, a monk of Scourmont who even with the intention of assuring for himself a more normal type of life would withdraw from the community, even if it were to go to another monastery, my conduct as Abbot would be as follows: I would not cry anathema at him, but I would refuse him my paternal blessing.

Consequently, my pressing exhortation to all of you will always remain as follows: maintain unity, keep the community together, stay with the community in dependence on the hierarchy. Remain as a family, in fraternal fellowship, united to the head, united among brothers. Let us not forget that for most of us this is the most easy and sure way to remain faithful to our monastic obligations.

It is not enough to maintain the community as a body, we must also maintain the spirit of Scourmont, our conception of contemplative life.

In the present circumstances, while respecting the Usages at their correct value, we have understood that they are not what is essential in our life. The activities of the contemplative life are these: celebration of the Office, prayer, reading and study, together with manual work as a source of earning our living.

Lastly, it is likewise necessary to preserve the particular spirit of our monastery. This spirit can vary according to the times,

> or with different superiors. Nevertheless, as long as an authorized and different line of direction is not given, we should keep to what constitutes our concept of life, our way of thinking.
>
> If circumstances do not permit us to observe absolute silence, let us know how to avoid banalities in our conversations and give our speaking together the character of monastic colloquies.
>
> I wish for each one of you that our Paschal communion on this last Holy Thursday may be a true communion with Christ, the Universal Church, and the Church of Scourmont in its body and soul. Amen.

The community was scarcely established in the château at Chimay when the occupation authorities informed them that they had reserved that place for themselves. The monks then considered moving to Brûly, where a generous benefactor of the community put his summer residence at the monk's disposition. Once again, the Germans opposed this by their veto. Their maliciousness became evident. The psychological tension in the community increased, and their discussions were full of confusion. The Father Abbot "*tractat apud se,*" as the Rule of Saint Benedict recommends. He devoted several hours to solitary reflection, and then drew up "directions on the political attitude which the religious of Scourmont Abbey should maintain." This text is worth quoting "*in extenso*" because of the clearness of its ideas, the soundness of its political analysis and the finesse of its religious understanding.

> It seems to me that it is necessary, in the present conditions, for the community and each of its members to have a clear idea of the attitude we should have in our judgments and in our acts toward the authority of the State, as well as toward the civil and military authorities who occupy and are in charge of the administration of Belgium. For this reason, we want to establish seven directive principles and rules to follow. In that way, once our position is clearly defined, we ask each one to have the determination and courage to conform to them in practice.

1. We should never lose sight of the fact that, as members of a religious community, we involve or risk to involve this community by simply expressing our opinions or by our exterior actions. That holds good even when it is a question of purely personal opinions or acts which concern no one but oneself. These implicate the reputation of the whole body of which we are all members. In fact, people easily attribute to the whole body what is proper to one of its members. Consequently, there is an obligation for each one of us to be prudent and cautious in the way he expresses his opinions and in his exterior actions.

2. Monks and religious, we are above all men of the Church. Our first country is the Church. The first State authority who rules us is the ecclesiastical authority. Because of this we are not exempt from civil authority, but we are obliged to make judgments and act with regard to this civil authority in the way that the Church understands and wishes. Now, it is the intention and wish of the Church that clergymen should not take the initiative in trends of thought or in political action. The Church wants and intends that religious should refrain absolutely from getting involved in political strife and stay away from all competition that is purely political. Likewise, and for the same reason, we are first of all Catholics before being citizens of a nation. Our interests are first of all of a Catholic nature. Our affection extends first to those who are Catholics, wherever they may be, from wherever they come, to the extent that they themselves put their being a Catholic above their political interests. It is for this motive, for example, that a soldier who belongs to an enemy or occupying army—even though he may be implicated in things we do not approve of—retains his right to our spiritual fraternity as soon as he presents himself to us as a Catholic.

3. By our life in this world we are incorporated in a nation, by birth or by where we reside. Because of this we are members of a civil society, of a state. Consequently, to the state which rules this nation we owe dependence, deference and obedience, unless the state commands something

which is contrary to either God's will or the rights of the Church. So we are all members of the community of Notre-Dame de Scourmont and we belong to the Belgian nation, even if all of us do not possess the juridical status of Belgian citizen. As such, we all desire freedom and Belgium's independence; we adopt by our judgment and even with affection the orders of the King, the only legitimate head of the Belgian State. And especially, in the present circumstances, we disapprove of all movements and actions of dissent. We refuse our esteem to persons who stir up such dissent or foster it by governmental attempts, whether by campaigns of opinion or in print. Besides, we have only to follow the enlightened directions given by the Cardinal Primate of Belgium in his pastoral letter of May 31, 1940: "As for us," said the illustrious prelate, "knowing that we agree with the almost unanimous sentiments of the throng of Belgian people, we maintain our respect, our faithfulness and our confidence with regard to our King . . . We desire that all Belgians, conscious of the seriousness of the present hour, remain united to and in agreement with the King, the supreme personification of the Fatherland in danger." Among the duties which our fidelity to the King—the only legitimate chief of the Belgian State—imposes upon us, it is proper to point out the obligation in which we find ourselves to accept and fulfill with loyalty the conditions laid down on May 28, 1941, in the protocol of the armistice. We therefore do not want to commit any act contrary to loyal acceptance of the armistice, either by information or activity in favor of any army whatsoever.

4. Confronted by the forces which occupy Belgian territory: we retain first of all the right to judge in our conscience the moral value of this occupation, according to the principles of God's law, of international law and the laws of the Belgian nation. We accord bodily and exterior obedience to the occupying forces, which does not impinge upon our loyalty to the King. As Cardinal Mercier said in his pastoral letter of December 25, 1914: "In themselves, the occupying army's acts of public administration would

have no force, but legitimate authority tacitly ratifies those acts which are justified because of their general interest, and their entire juridical value ensues from this ratification alone." Because of these motives, we submit to the occupying authority in the spheres of political, military, economic and social matters, and in everything that is not essential to the ecclesiastic or monastic life. Each professed member who has stability in the community of Notre-Dame de Scourmont should take to heart, by fidelity to his profession, to stay in the place where he has made his stability and to have the courage, if he should meet with opposition to these rights, to preserve a bond with the community and its established hierarchy. Apart from these rights and guidelines, we will abstain from controversies and contradictions among ourselves or with the occupying personnel about details concerning the occupation and how things are going. Once again: our condition as a monk and a man of the Church obliges us to be reserved, prudent and circumspect in the way we look at political happenings, and to be more preoccupied with giving priority to what is spiritual. Silence, without servile acquiescence, without loud opposition, is the worthiest line of conduct in these circumstances. Following Cardinal Mercier's good advice: "Let us respect the rulings which the occupying forces impose on us, as long as they do not infringe upon the freedom of our Christian consciences or our patriotic dignity. Let us not try to make courage consist of bravado, nor bravery turn to agitation. You, especially, my dear colleagues in the priesthood, be at the same time the best guardians of patriotism and supporters of public order. In the domain of thought and culture, a special mention should be made of some consequences that are frequent when there is triumph by arms. The success of a State's power tends to make everything that comes from that state dominate in people's minds: the political form, intellectual culture, conceptions of art and customs. We should beware of being swept along in a servile way. A free and healthy sense of judgment keeps intact prudence, which does not cease to evaluate things according to their intrinsic value and not according to the craze of the present moment."

5. Before someone in the occupying troops who carries out orders, that is to say, before the soldier or even before a local authority, we should bear in mind that they are not responsible for the acts that come from the authority that gives the orders, but that they are simply men who are accomplishing a duty imposed upon them, which they cannot avoid because of their origin and their nationality. So in our relationships with them we conduct ourselves as we do with guests, treating them in a completely human way, to use the expression in the Rule of Saint Benedict, particularly if they are bound to us by Catholic, or even Christian, brotherhood. In this sense, in our relations we adopt the customs which are usual among men: greeting them in the ordinary way without any indication of adhesion to a party, that is, offering a sincere hand shake. We should excuse and even understand that there is a difference in the way of judging things and events. Statements which we think are biased, or orders, do not require any answer or rectification from us. Silence in the face of an affirmation by someone who is speaking to us is not an approval of or consent to what is said.

6. Toward the other nations, especially toward those who are engaged in the conflict: It is useless to insist on the freedom that we possess to keep the feelings of preference we have because of our origin, our relations, or because of the cause they stand for. The good of the Church is the measure of our preferences. Pity for a country in distress, even if it is not our homeland, is a Christian sentiment.

7. A special rule should be made about the attitude we should take with regard to information concerning the war, general information about judgments, about facts themselves, or even more so, about what is published concerning real facts or alleged facts. In general, publicity about events, in spite of easy circulation and reception today, is warped by the interests of those in charge of it and biased commentators. The truth about facts and the significance of events is difficult to figure out. For this reason, we think that it is prudent not to listen to everything that is published. We want to continue in the line of conduct we

> adopted at the beginning of the war, that is to say: We do not receive any newspaper, of whatever tendency it may be, and we do not listen to anything on the radio, no matter where it comes from. We can make an exception only for official information, such as orders coming from authority, notices from ecclesiastic authority, or direct publication of legal documents and decrees coming from the civil authority.

After months of insecurity and real suffering for Dom Anselme, the community ended up in the "gloomy crossroads" of Momignies, with the Christian Brothers. It was not an ideal place for monks, obliged as they were to live side by side with a colony of youngsters who occupied a large part of the abandoned boarding school. With humble discretion the Father Abbot gave his recommendations to his monks:

> We, Brother Anselme Le Bail, Abbot of Notre-Dame de Scourmont, to our brothers exiled in this place, we ask you to observe the same discretion as our host.
>
> In the Constitution of Notre-Dame de Scourmont in exile at Momignies, issued on April 19, 1942, we declared: "As to our residence, as to our use of the buildings, the community of Notre-Dame de Scourmont is the guest of the Christian Brothers of Momignies. From these provisional circumstances there result for us new duties and new dependence. To the Christian Brothers, to the Reverend Brother Director of Momignies, the community of Notre-Dame de Scourmont owes thanks: the thanks of guests, which goes over and beyond that of tenants. The community also owes reverence and attentiveness to the persons who offer us hospitality, and to their desires. Our condition as guests in the boarding school of Momignies obliges us likewise to respect the quarters that are put at our disposition. This respect ought to be expressed by our carefulness not to cause the deterioration of anything, and not to use or change anything without the consent of those who are in charge of this place."
>
> That is what we wrote on April 19 of this year. Since that time, the Reverend Brother Director has obligingly repeated that he graciously placed these lodgings at our disposition

> without wanting to ask for any payment, just as he has put other quarters at the disposition of "Foyer Leopold III."
>
> As for practical details, we declare and we give the following directions:
>
> 1. Any new occupation of parts of the buildings, any new use of material objects belonging to the boarding school should be arranged with the Reverend Brother Director.
> 2. Any change, any re-arrangement which has to do with the places already occupied should be authorized by the agreement of the Reverend Brother Director.
> 3. To maintain order and unity, all desires, all requests concerning these two points should be presented to Father Prior, who alone will deal with the Reverend Brother Director.
> 4. For occasional or temporary use of tools, material, or other things used for the upkeep of the school, it suffices to speak to the dear Brother in charge of maintenance.
>
> Given at Momignies, July 4, 1942.

All the same, the monks had use of a chapel for themselves, a very suitable study room, several quite large rooms, and a small vegetable garden. They observed the Usages and Customs as well as they could; this was not Dom Anselme's principal preoccupation. For him, what was most important was to maintain a stable fraternal community united with its Abbot.

As in many other circumstances of his life, during this 5-year long exile Dom Le Bail also showed himself to be at the same time a man of audacious imagination and cordiality. Beginning in September, 1939, he launched *"The monk-soldier, Bulletin of Cistercians in the Army."* He explained:

> All the professed religious of Notre-Dame de Scourmont who have been called up are asked to send their military address to the Reverend Father Abbot. They should also write every time they are transferred. It is proper for them to give news of themselves more often. The community wants to be kept up to date on the situation of each one. In that way, their interest, charity and devotedness will be kept alive.

> All the enlisted men who are professed religious of Notre-Dame de Scourmont should give an account of the money they have received and of their expenditures. The Reverend Father Abbot authorizes each one to receive pay and to spend what he judges proper for a religious. In his account of his expenditures he should indicate in a summarized way the nature of these expenditures, especially if they have not been made for food or other needs for his living.
>
> The Abbey provides packages for soldiers who have been called up. Father Columban is in charge of this service: address your desires directly to him.

When the war was over, in the last issue of the Bulletin, Dom Anselme was proud and happy to summarize:

> The "Monk-Soldier" of Notre-Dame de Scourmont has conquered the evils of war.
>
> War, in spite of its legitimacy and moral nobility insofar as it raises the citizen to the rank of being a witness to what is right—even to the point of giving one's life—, brings with it the evils of broken-up families and the dispersion of their members. It can cause division and even discord among hearts, in the very interests of legitimate defense.
>
> The Monks of Scourmont did not refuse the benefit of the war. The monk-soldiers of Scourmont, thirty in number—and even for a while as many as 43 out of a total of 84 members—joined their military stations and served very honorably.
>
> All the Scourmont monks endured the hardships of war and dispersion, as well as evacuation of the monastery (three times), partial division of the community, imprisonment of 11 of their brothers, and internment in camps.
>
> Dispersion, separation, all the evils of war, the monks of Scourmont have vanquished all of them every day during the course of the years 1939/1945. Uninterruptedly, in their hearts and in their acts they have preserved the unity of the family body in the unity of the spirit.

28

The monastic adventure in warm terms

During his Chapters, Sundays, weekly or daily, the Abbot of a monastery knows that he has before him "an indocile and restive flock" (according to Saint Benedict), whose strongest monks expect to be encouraged to go further, and whose weakest hope not to be discouraged. The Abbot knows therefore that he should show discretion, the mother of virtues, a discretion which forbids him to say everything which he "has on his heart." But what he "has in his heart," the Abbot courageously expresses on the occasion of a profession, temporary or solemn, to monks "young in age" or "newcomers" in the monastic life. They are still able to hear and accept strong words, without the deafening parasites of wear and tear, scepticism, fatigue or mental reservations.

Dom Le Bail was one of those abbots who in such special circumstances loved to let his heart overflow, speaking directly to the newly professed, and addressing the majority of the flock in indirect terms.

Here we publish several sermons given by the Father Abbot Anselme at profession ceremonies between 1930 and 1940. We have chosen five sermons, five great and majestic frescoes of the monastic adventure.

The first sermon dates from 1934. Dom Anselme delivered this sermon before four young monks scarcely 21 years old, who had just pronounced their temporary vows. The Father Abbot took advantage of this occasion to develop the theme of the excellence of giving oneself to God in one's youth. Pommeled today by human, psycho-sociological science, we are tempted to have a kind of suspicion with regard to quite young candidates who present themselves at the gate of our monasteries. And usually, it is wise for us to do so. But Dom Le Bail's warm confidence can also rekindle our too chilly prudence.

> Your group of four novices who entered the monastery together, your youth, your passing directly from college to the cloister, are like so many factors which invite me to consider the aspect "gift" which monastic Profession implies, an aspect which is common to all monks, but which is particular to young monks. The gift of self by vows is all the more pleasing to God when it is made in one's youth.
>
> From a natural point of view, youth is the age of grace. There is something in young people which makes them love spontaneously. We love the rising of the sun, whereas it is nothing if it does not reach the hour of noon. We love spring flowers, but there again, they are nothing if they do not bear fruit in summer. But it is not about these things that I want to speak.
>
> Here I am thinking of the aspect of gift which takes on a very special quality in young people, as if youth was the ideal age for the total gift of self: the quality of giving one's life from the beginning, as soon as one can dispose of oneself. That is pleasing to our human regard; that is pleasing to God's eyes. This gift can of course begin with Baptism, but it is with full consciousness and his intelligence that the young religious gives himself. It is a consecration to God of one's conscious life, in the perspective of duration. It is not what is superfluous that one should offer to God but the first fruits. In the divine Law of the Old Testament, the first fruits were offered to God. The gift of the first-born signified that God took possession of the family. This donation was not necessarily accompanied by consecration of one's entire life, but it was always an acknowledgement of God's sovereignty.
>
> Among the four ages of life, youth is not the preference of poets. They attribute more value to the age of maturity and old age, the ages of experience and prudent decisions. It is true that for governing the world, the qualities required are not generally found among the young.
>
> But the specific quality of youth is the promptitude which is perfectly suited to a gift. At the age of maturity one has a

tendency to calculate, to become stingy. But youth is not stingy, it does not know how to hold back, its gift is beyond all measure. What could be considered to be lack of reflection is in this case the very quality of a gift, a total gift by forgetfulness of self. And with joy: "*Hilarem datorem diligit Deus.*" (God loves one who gives with joy). Youth loves to please, and God finds in it his pleasure.

To all these qualities of a youthful gift, however, in your case we must add another one, that of a certain maturity which already allows you to be very conscious of what you are committing yourself to. You began to acquire this maturity through your classical studies, by your knowledge of different surroundings, your involvement in youth movements, your participation in study groups, which have taught you to observe, judge correctly and act more than to talk. You have deepened this comprehension of life during your two years of novitiate, and you must continue in this line so that your gift may be fully human: complete donation, joyful and intelligent, because more than the quantity of the gift, it is the understanding of the gift which glorifies God.

I must, however, add a terrible reflection; because He loves the gift of youth, it happens that God replies to it by the gift of death. It happens that an abbot sometimes wishes the death of his young religious. It is terrible to think that. And yet, when one looks at the history of souls, one is sometimes tempted to pray: "O God, take him quickly, for his holiness and salvation, because he could one day take back the total gift made this day." And sometimes the gift of eternal springtime is granted. If we compare Saint Thérèse of the Child Jesus with Saint Thomas Aquinas or Bernard, what difference of graces! The saints who die young please humanity and win people's devotion.

I do not wish you to die young. It is a manner of saying that, by its aspect of rupture, monastic Profession offers to the gift of self stability in eternal youth. That is what we all ought to wish for ourselves (Temporary Profession, September 8, 1934.)

The second sermon also dates from 1934. Dom Anselme preached it before a monk somewhat older who was going to make his solemn vows. As counterpoint to his preceding sermon, on the excellence of giving oneself to God in youth, the Father

Abbot developed the theme of man's mysterious wandering until he finally finds his place of human and spiritual stability. Here also, Dom Le Bail makes a connection with situations current today in our monasteries, where men "who have lived" knock at the door. Here also, his words help us to welcome with respect and hope these "new arrivals" who are no longer young.

When I think of the long road, in space and time, that you have travelled to arrive at La Trappe, I would like to mention a point which concerns the whole of humanity: it takes lots of time to arrive at settling one's life, to discover a bright light which shines on the itinerary of one's whole existence. Equador, India, Holland, Belgium, literary studies, a well-established career, very honorable before man and before God!

And finally, you arrived at Scourmont! It was a new birth which took you back to childhood. You had to become a child again in the novitiate, and also sitting on the bench of the Roman school, where the schedule at the Generalate obliges one to be a child even more than in the monastery. It is one's whole life that has been made over. From your personal adventure there appears an established fact that occurs in the life of many men: the desire to acquire stability. Being on the road is really an astonishing phenomenon. One has perhaps fallen, but that was just weakness, and one does not abandon the route because one has fallen there.

The real reason for our astonishment is this insecurity that a man experiences until he has made up his mind about his destiny. Is man not the most unstable of living beings, the most errant among the creatures on our earth? In the field of politics, everyone today is revolutionary. People discover that the former ways of doing things are not the right ones. They hunt for others, and insecurity increases and persists. Where is the world going? In one's personal life, it is the same thing. Today philosophers and writers amuse themselves with the sweetness of doubt, smile on the soft pillow of doubt, with a kind of anguished irony.

So, where to settle down? In the world or in the cloister? Or rather: wander around the world or take one's abode in God? The question has to do with happiness: where will I be the most happy? The answer is sometimes a vivid flash, when the light appears in one's youth. In that case, what peace it is to choose God immediately! But what anguish when the instability goes on and creates insecurity as the time comes for one to decide.

Dear brother, today you have decided to abide in stability in the cloister. And you are in peace. Even so, you are not yet at the end of the road. A new road is opening up before you. And to travel it, there must be a light to guide your footsteps. In today's world, as you know very well, each person claims to be his own light. This pretension is not necessarily inexact, as long as a person clearly understands of what light it is a question. In our Cistercian tradition, it is a question of true knowledge of self.

But knowledge of myself begins with knowledge of man in general: how does the soul conduct itself in its relation with itself, with others, with God? We come back to Saint Bernard's triple "Consideration": consideration of self which leads to compunction; consideration of others which leads to mercy; consideration of God which leads to contemplation. Aelred, Isaac and other Cistercian Fathers always thought that there was no way to make a monk except by first placing him before the possibilities and limits of the soul. One does not become a monk by a call from heaven or by the commands of an authority. One chooses to become a monk after "consideration" of the psychological possibilities of the soul. Then only can one decide if one is capable of undertaking the ascent of the spiritual ladder.

And as soon as one has committed oneself, one receives enough light to continue. There will of course be nights, and dark nights. But one should not think that it is perfection to be in these nights. The human spirit is not made to exist in nights. We must not glorify the "obscure nights." There is, certainly, a night of the senses, a night that we want. That is to say, by our own decision we want to go beyond the sweetness of the imagination and senses in order to approach the invisible. There is a night of the spirit, a night that we willfully desire when we refuse to rely on our reason alone and trust in the intelligence of faith and the intuition of love. These nights, in spite of their name, are not paths of darkness.They are simple ways to find our way out of darkness and come into the light.

> After having established the place and form of its stability, the soul should seek its dogma, its personal light. At the Gregorian you have of course studied the dogmas of Catholic theology. But these are not the ones which have guided you personally, like a continual catechism or an uninterrupted course. You have to have a personal dogma, a light which is your own. This is a special study, a directing dogma for your soul. This personal dogma, the fruit of your deliberate choice, is a source of life, consolation and light for the soul.
>
> The monk draws this light from his conversations with God. This contemplative prayer is of course not a parlor where people speak. Our personal prayer is not made up of established themes, as in a circle for studies: it repeats banalities, formulas which linger in our memory; it expresses the conditions of our soul which are often nothing but laments of our weakness and misery. It is in this crucible that a monk can find his path and his light. To the question: "What is your way?" never be satisfied with answering—as though you had learned a lesson—that it is your needs and observances. Answer in a personal way, referring to the living light which enlightens your own path.
>
> Happy is the soul who sees clearly on his path, who understands the reason for his existence, and who goes along simply and quietly because he is sure of his destination! He is joyful then as if he possessed the goal already. The possession of the end is nothing but the present assurance of the goal and of the road which leads to it. There peace is found, the peace which I wish you, my brother.

The third sermon dates from April 29, 1936, the occasion of a solemn profession on the feast of Saint Peter of Verona, a Dominican religious and martyr. In it, Dom Anselme developed the traditional relationship between the monastic life and martyrdom. In his time it was widely thought that Christian monastic life replaced martyrdom, which had disappeared with the Edict of Constantine. Today, in a more nuanced way, it is thought that the monastic movement was born instead during the very period of fervor of the Church of the martyrs. Dom Le Bail never limited himself by hypotheses, and simply echoed the Tradition according to which, by virginity and obedience, the monastic life can be compared to the patient fervor of martyrdom.

There is a long tradition that a link exists between the monastic life and martyrdom. Not that entering the monastery means condemnation to death. Not that monastic Profession is a wish to undergo martyrdom. Not that becoming a monk implies that one is surrendering one's body to intolerable torments. Not that the monastic life resembles a destructive holocaust of the human person. No, none of all that.

If traditionally there is a link between the monastic life and martyrdom, it is the link of virginity. At a time when, because of the fact that the Church had become officially recognized, the frequency and possibility of martyrdom diminished, Christians wanted to give witness to their total donation to Christ, body and soul, by virginity. In both cases, martyrdom and virginity can go without a verbal confession of faith. In both cases, the silent gift of self suffices. There have been epochs and places when it was rather the vow of obedience which seemed to signify the gift of self, that is to say, the fact of entrusting oneself to another, with humility and patience. There were epochs and places when it was the vow of virginity which seemed to express best the gift of self to Christ.

And here we must not look upon virginity in the narrow way of thinking—still too widespread—as renouncement of sexual and affective life. It should be considered in its large and positive sense, of loving and complete consecration to Christ.

Here we are in the presence of two different ways of looking at human life. Two different ways of looking, not that in the moral sense one is better than the other. But different in the symbolic sense, one not signifying the same thing as the other.

On one side, someone who chooses marriage, with its affective, sexual and familial dimension, replies to the fundamental need of man to perpetuate himself: to perpetuate himself by children, establish a freehold, develop the well-being of the little society which he has founded, educate it, raise it, improve its social welfare. It is a legitimate vocation, and besides, one willed by the Creator, insofar as one does not forget the spiritual dimension of this vocation. If this dimension is not there, one loses oneself in gests of instinctive passion, pleasure, the sole preoccupation of making money and preparing a glorious future for one's descendents. What was at the beginning a vocation to openness to the Spirit, can develop into being locked up in the flesh.

On the other hand, someone who chooses virginity with all its dimensions of solitude, awakens the desire hidden in the heart of man: that of eternal life. It is, of course, this desire for eternity that spouses and parents attempt to express, an eternal life intended and hoped for later. Virgins, monks and nuns, avow that they have already attained eternity, since they have gone beyond the intermediaries of married and family life.

But the monk, the nun, must also be a virgin with conviction and honesty. It is not possible for a monk to settle down in his "celibate state," repeating the customs of certain centuries when a boy entered the monastery so as not to reduce the family patrimony, or where the young girl became a nun because she didn't have a dowry. Those types of virginity have nothing in common with a martyr's witness. Revolutions were not wrong when they burned down such monasteries.

Yes, the state of virginity does not suffice as a witness. There must be added to it the intimate and practical conviction that it is a loving gift of self to Christ. A spontaneous donation, more important even than the patient donation by obedience.

And yet, we must come back again for a moment to obedience as another dimension of martyrdom. It is legitimate, for all men and even for all Christians, to have the freedom to dispose of themselves, to make choices and to plan their future. Did the God of Genesis not make man his co-creator and the gardener of his earth? Still, man must accept to be a prince and not a sovereign, not to think his power comes from himself, and to remain an obedient subject of his Creator. Consequently, the monk—by his very title of being a religious—makes profession of the virtue of religion, that is to say that he wants to attribute to God what is due to Him, by his dependence on Him. He renounces all freedoms, even legitimate ones, to establish himself in absolute dependence and in this way acknowledge by his whole life the primacy of God. When obedience includes all the acts of daily life, even to those of least importance, when it is lived continually "under a Rule and an Abbot," when it follows in everything the orders and judgments of others (*"ambulans alieno iudicio et imperio"*), it gives witness that man is not his own master, that he is subject and dependent, and that God is the first Principle and ruler of the universe.

This is how the monastic life is a twofold martyrdom: by virginity and obedience. But this martyrdom usually does not lead to anticipation of anything bloody. And it is true that making profession avoids many risks: one will never lack anything necessary, one will not have worries about money; one will never be troubled by family problems or a professional career. But then, how much more should we double our generosity and honesty in our vocation of virginity and obedience! We ought to assume in silence our suffering from being alone—by our vow of virginity—, and of being dependent—by our vow of obedience. The Church needs our humble and silent preaching.

The fourth Sermon dates from October 3, 1937, on the occasion of the simple profession of two young monks. Dom Le Bail developed a theme which was dear to him, that of relationships between what is exterior and what is interior, in the Cistercian pedagogy.

My dear sons, you know that Saint Bernard had to deal with the controversy about knowing which monk observes the Rule best. But this question—we know very well—is not limited only to the time of Saint Bernard: it comes up in every epoch, and today too, because it concerns what is characteristically human. The question is, in fact, to know if it is the body which forms and rules the spirit, or if it is rather the spirit which governs and forms the body. Let us remark, however, that the question has to do with the indisputable respective dignity of both the body and the spirit. It consists in knowing what, in the formation of man, should have priority: exterior discipline or the life of the spirit.

Discipline is made up of perceptible things: rules, observances, the framework of one's life, ways of doing things. We think that certainly, by their redundancy and rebounding, both form the soul, seeing that the body and soul remain together and influence each other mutually. But the question is about which is to have the priority: is it discipline which should have the chief place in education and draw the soul along; or is it the spirit which should be given preference, forming then the body to its image?

This question will always be disputed.

It came up already in the time of the first Christians: Is it the Law of the commandments or that of the Spirit which makes a man just? It was raised by the first monks who chose the first answer: the best monk is the one who observes the letter of the discipline perfectly and beats the records of fasting and penance. As to Saint Benedict, he leaned toward the second reply, in that he recommended moderation of austerity and exterior discipline, in order to offer the soul all its chances to be at ease and arrive at liberty of the spirit.

As a matter of fact, this question is not proper to monastic Profession. For a Christian, every profession requires the gift of all one's being to God, body and soul. So it is that the duty to serve people in the civil society is accompanied by disciplinary rules. The monk—he also—, when he promises "conversion of his ways," commits himself to submit to a certain discipline of life, which the Rule and the Usages and Customs interpret. This is indisputable: it is a contract which has to do with sensible realities. And people respect such contracts.

What can be debated is the pedagogy: by what kind of pedagogy can one succeed in forming novices to observe the Rule most fervently? Let us examine the two opinions:

The first opinion encourages that priority be given to what is corporal, to exterior conduct and to a pattern of living. It is founded on the conviction that nothing can touch the spirit which has not first of all passed by the intermediary of the senses. In education and formation, one will be vigilant about the priority of exterior practice of observances. And the novitiate, in particular, becomes principally a school of exterior observances. This conception exists in the Order and among us.

From this prime importance given to observances there results, of course, the extreme difficulty not only of conceding but even inventing dispenses, dispenses from the Office in choir, from the dietary rules, from the time set aside for reading, from manual work and from other obligations of the Rule. It doesn't make any difference, for example, if one falls asleep in the morning in the Scriptorium: what is important is to be there, with one's book in front of him. Let us not accuse this conception of the monastic life as being pharisaism: it translates the conviction that exterior observance has an influence on the spiritual and even provokes it. Here, it is the virtue of religion, as you learned in the novitiate: consecration of our corporal being to God is rightly and already adoration, and the intention—even though not always conscious and effective at the present time—is in any case, fundamental: to do everything for love of God.

To this first opinion we are permitted to prefer the second, according to which we encourage priority given to the spirit; not that the spirit, as such, claims superiority over matter, but because we believe that it is from the spirit that strict and pure observance flows necessarily, by superabundance. Here it is equally a question of the virtue of religion, by which the novice discovers that he is nothing but an effect, in relationship to his God, first Principle; and that he is only a subject, in relation to his God, Sovereign Master.

These truths hold good, no doubt, for all men, but religious consecrate themselves specially and exclusively to live them with conviction. Application of the virtue of religion is therefore the principal occupation in the novitiate, to be continued moreover during one's whole religious life by reflection, meditation, and examination of conscience on this subject. As for exterior acts, they will follow, necessarily by this spirit of religion.

If great knowledge of the virtue of religion, and of its principal act, are not translated into exterior acts, we could, equally and correctly, call it pharisaism. Plenitude requires acts, and first of all the act of devotion, which includes everything, by subjecting the will to God. Devotion is not yet an act of obedience, but this disposition of our whole being to yield to what God wants. Just as a runner ready to go at the signal, his hands already touching the ground, straining toward the goal, toward the accomplishment of what will be God's service.

The value of this method, which we prefer to the first opinion, is not founded on the fact that a man is a reasonable creature, but on the realization that it produces an observance superior to the Rule. Referring to the chapter on humility in the Rule, Saint Bernard asked himself which monk is more observant: the one who is most tired, the one who is most worn out, or the most humble? Obviously, the most humble, that is to say, the one who excels in everything which applies to the virtue of religion.

This pedagogy wins out over the first opinion for still another reason: it is, that the observances can change, one can be excused or dispensed from them. Thus, when a monk is infirm or sick the practice of observances is dropped partially or completely. Is monastic profession dropped because of this? Does the duty to live as a religious disappear? A monk who is confined to bed, suffering, for twenty-five years ought to remain a religious, live his profession of the virtue of religion, subject to God in devotion, ready and prompt to will what God wills. That way he remains a religious perfectly. Because he wants the spirit of the Rule, he practices it truly to the letter.

This pedagogy is likewise more vast. So it is that sometimes charity imposes the duty to renounce practicing exterior observances; or in the case of war or expulsion from the cloister, should monastic observances be dropped? No. The monk soldier should maintain deep within himself what is essential: his religious profession, by devotion. So it is because it is larger that this pedagogy is superior to the other opinion, and not because it would be more rational.

You know all this teaching already, my dear sons. You are disposed to practice exteriorly the whole of the Rule: the conversion of your ways and stability, of course. But, above all, preserve what you have received in the novitiate, this knowledge of the virtue of religion, by which you will live up to your profession perfectly.

The fifth sermon dates from October 24, 1940. The Second World War had broken out in May. The community of Scourmont was already deprived of 46 monks who had been called up for the war. The Father Abbot had before him two of his monks who were about to make their solemn vows, students at Rome, whose work towards their doctorate had been interrupted by the worldwide conflict. Dom Le Bail profited from this occasion to present his reflections on the pagan idea of totalitarianism of the state, and to clarify the distinction between studies in a university, which can be useful and necessary, and the studious application of each monk to the Search for Truth, in his seeking for God.

In the present circumstances, I cannot refrain from speaking about present events, in order to give a lesson to the community. Last April, when Brother Robert made solemn profession, I endeavored to distinguish what the substance of the monastic life is and what is accidental, in order to maintain, if possible, the substance in face of and contrary to everything else. And in face of and against the recent events and in spite of the departure of 46 religious who replied to the military call, you have maintained the bond with the dispersed community. Thanks to that, it is now reconstituted, not only in its substance but even in its "accidental form."

I must now analyze what is at stake in what is happening at present, not only from the angle of disturbances that these events cause concerning the organization of our monastic life, nor from the angle of occupation of territory and privation of freedoms. Fundamentally, what is at stake is what has to do with our way of looking at the world and human life.

On the one hand, we have the idea of "State-God," of "State-Everything," which affirms that man finds his goal in himself and himself alone, and that he is simply an element of the State. The State-God makes its own truth: since it is God, everything it says is True, Just, Holy: it suffices in itself and becomes man's final destiny.

On the other hand, we have the ancient Christian concept: man does not suffice in himself, he is dependent, on his way; he does not make truth, it is proposed to him and he should seek it; and holiness consists of conforming oneself to the divine will.

In the Middle Ages there was similar confrontation. On the one hand, in the form of chivalry, men succeeded in making man's goal valor and strength and quest of courtly love. Knighthood on this earth, completely centered on swords and the emotions of love, found its expression in the tales of Arthur, of the Round Table and the Search for the Holy Grail.

On the other hand, the Church opposes the spirit of the Gospel to the too human concept of chivalry, by favoring spiritual chivalry: "Hearken! Lord knight: let no one enter such an elevated service before he is cleansed and divested of all that is villainous and from all mortal sins. For this Quest has nothing to do with seeking earthly things, but seeking great secrets of

Our Lord and intimacy with him, and also the great "*repostailles*" that the Most High Master will show to the blessed knight whom he will have chosen among the other earthly knights." It was Saint Bernard who, in 1138, praised this new knighthood: (*De laude novae militiae*). It is he who proclaimed: "They leave, the Cistercian knights, who have taken the short cut to reach Jerusalem and find manifestly the revelation of the Holy Grail, that is to say, the discovery of God and man '*capax Dei*' (capable of God). And it was also he who said in his first Sermon for Lent: "We enter, dear brothers, into the Christian Knighthood."

You also, my brothers, by your solemn profession, set out on a great adventure, the quest of the Holy Grail, that is to say, seeking the revelation of Our Lord's secrets and God's "*repostailles.*" Your profession is your dubbing as knights. And on the occasion of your setting out, I want to give you a few pointers so that you may succeed in your Quest. Today I am going to stress an aspect which seems to me to be important: the "search" for divine Truth, by assiduous study. You are studying at Roman universities and you seem to be on your way to becoming doctors in something or other, unless present events make you simply "aborted" doctors. But what difference does it make after all, as long as, through all that, you seek Divine truth. "Pursue through all that" means that this laborious knowledge is a type of ascesis motivated by loving seeking for God." *Amor ipse notitia est* (love itself is properly speaking knowledge). I do not see you yielding to the temptation of thinking of your monastic life as only applying yourselves to study. What is at stake is not the greater or lesser importance of "studies," but rather the fundamental and irreplaceable importance "of the study," that is to say, the untiring quest for God, intense application of "*cogitatio*" to discover the Truth. A triple Truth, or more exactly, a single Truth made up of three aspects of knowledge: of self, of one's neighbor, of God, and the relationship of these three to each other.

The first quest consists in seeking to know what a human being is, to discover the truth which is proper to him. In the account of the *Quest for the Holy Grail*, there is an error at the outset. The Knights set out with earthly impetuosity, and they do not succeed because of their exaggerated confidence in their strength. A Cistercian monk warns them: "The Holy Grail is the grace of the Holy Spirit." To Gauvain, Hector, Melyant, Lancelot, he said: "To take up Christ's shield is to be patient and learn humility." Lancelot, a true "preudhomme" (honest man), learned the lesson and accepted to ride a donkey, a very ridiculous little mount, but Christ's mount. "To be Christ's mount," Saint Bernard said in a Sermon for the feast of Saint Benedict ("*Pium iumentum Christi sumus*"). In his commentary on the Degrees of Humility of the Rule of Saint Benedict, Saint Bernard wrote that the first step in the quest is knowledge of self, "the most true of the virtues, by which man, by knowledge of self, recognizes that he is of little worth (*vilescit*). Thus, humiliation is the first way of humility, a way which requires the human effort of reason, "consideration," that is, "intense study applied to seeking" (*intensa ad investigandum cogitatio*).

In the tradition of Cîteaux, this study was applied not only to knowledge of the soul ("*De anima*"), but also of the body ("*De corpore*"). Because we must know first of all what man is if we are to approach the question of his possible relationships with God: how can man—the soul, the spirit and the senses—how can he reach God? Man is "*capax Dei*" (capable of God): yes, but how? We understand: here, it is already the Quest for likeness. This step is that of consideration on human love.

According to Saint Bernard, in fact, when man believes that God is Charity, he ought to understand that his capacities to love, to turn freely towards someone or something, reveal to him that he has a capacity for God. This is human love which changes into divine love.

To make this work of resemblance easier, we can look upon Christ, Christ in his mysteries, Christ, perfect Image of God available to human beings.

These are the steps of monastic study par excellence. Other types of study are useful, legitimate, praiseworthy, necessary. But if present events oblige you to interrupt them, you will always be able, like your brothers who are prisoners, to pursue your studious Quest as monks. "*Quaerit anima Verbum,*" Saint Bernard has told you. (Solemn Profession October 24, 1940).

29

When will there be time to sit down?

During the World War II exile, Dom Anselme was able to maintain the observances, if not integrally, at least what is essential in monastic obligations and the spirit of the Rule. A proof of this was the zeal and untiring devotedness shown by all the monks when it was time to return to life in the Abbey, and to assume once again all the monastic observances.

There was plenty to do to put things back into order. Financially the Abbey was ruined, and at the same time it was necessary to modernize all the industrial and farm equipment. Dom Anselme was tired out. He wrote to his brother-in-law:

> At 70, I feel like I am 100! This weight does not consist of a groaning body but in feeling the burden of responsibilities. Each day brings its trouble, its difficulty, and with age a person is more sensitive, more upset by the troubles of others . . . Thirty-five years as abbot! I dream of having some time for retirement, like you. In the meantime, I travel on business, always on business, no pleasure . . .
>
> I let you know that I am in the class of old people in the Order: I am 70 years old since last December 31, the last day of my youth. Youth is gone, it is time to sit down, it is time to be an old man. I am an old man. It is difficult for me to believe it. I still have the consolation of thinking that Eternal Life will be an eternal youth. But the present is counted in years. Today, I put myself in the rank of old men.

On Monday, March 14, 1949, after celebrating a late Lenten Mass in community—a service which he liked to render in order to lighten the burden of fasting for the hebdomadary—, the Father Abbot suddenly collapsed at his work table. Still, it was not yet death. Death would make him wait seven long years. He was cared for very devotedly by his monks—especially his faithful monk-nurse—who were at his side with their filial and discreet affection right up until the end. As for him, he never complained. Accustomed to suffering, he usually was smiling in a way that was more teasing than resigned. Still, there was no doubt about his realizing his state, at least enough to experience his physical and intellectual decline. But his heart remained very alive: one could see that each morning, when one of the monks brought him Holy Communion.

On Tuesday, September 25, 1956, at 2:30 in the morning—he was 77 years and 8 months old—his Lord called him to eternal joys.

30

Let the enigma cease and day break!

Life is like a day, from morning until evening,
Beyond is the night, this immense silence
So simple and dense and pure that one can know nothing about it.

His finger sealing his lips, close by,
The angel of the great crossing is there waiting for me
To lead my life to another existence.

When he will smile at me it will be the moment,
He will come to untie the mooring cable,
The dream will end with the end of time.

I will turn back a little toward the wake
Where voices, glances will still hold me back,
I will weep no doubt, seeing some faces . . .

Then everything will be veiled by the shadow of death
Until suddenly, as in another dream,
Everything will be transfigured, both hearts and bodies . . .

Oh! Let the enigma cease and may the Day break.

C. D.

Epilogue

Few men have had a greater influence on the Cistercian Order of the Strict Observance than Dom Anselme Le Bail had during the first half of the twentieth century. Before exerting this influence at the General Chapter and in the various commissions created by the Chapter, he first influenced his own community and the rest of the Order through services rendered by monks formed at Scourmont.

In conformity with his motto *Abba, Pater*, Dom Anselme was first of all a father. He firmly believed in the grace of paternity he received at the moment he was chosen by his brothers to be their abbot, and he always looked at this spiritual paternity in the perspective of the pure spiritual tradition of Christianity. For him, to be a father consisted not of begetting spiritual sons for himself, but of bringing Christ forth in adult men who desired to let themselves be gradually transformed into the likeness of Christ through the use of the means furnished by monastic *conversatio*. These monks, who had freely chosen to live with brothers subject to a Rule and an abbot, were always invited and helped by him to reach full human and spiritual maturity; he encouraged them to act very freely in exercising their responsibilities.

It is this fundamental attitude which explains how he was able to have such an influence on his community, in spite of the exceptional circumstances which prevailed during his time as abbot: two world wars, each time with dispersion of the monks. Elected abbot in 1913, he himself left for the front on ambulance duty in 1914. After returning to the monastery in 1919, he spent almost the entire year of 1921 in Africa in order to accomplish a special mission assigned to him by the Order. This mission was followed by many others. But present or absent, it was always he who was truly the *abba* of Scourmont.

After making sure that they had received a solid monastic formation, he invited a number of his monks to develop their human and intellectual aptitudes in fields for which they had either a particular attraction or special aptitudes. This formation was always in view of service to the community or the Order. Even those whom he intended to assign to positions of material administration were sent out by him for advanced studies in theology. And he did this at a time when intellectual formation was not particularly well looked upon in the Order.

The Order had just recently emerged from a long "Observance War" between the Common and Strict Observances, followed by tensions scarcely more edifying among the various congregations which had arisen from the Reform of La Trappe. After the 1892 General Chapter, which united three of these congregations following the line of the Chapters of 1869 and 1891 which had united only the abbots of the Common Observance, the great Cistercian Order found itself henceforth divided into two parallel branches. It was a great temptation for each one of them to invest a considerable amount of energy defending their positions and justifying their decisions, appealing to historical and canonical arguments which in view of the complexity of the situation could always be used in whatever way they wanted. Dom Anselme avoided this snare and at the beginning adopted a position which was above this dispute. From the very outset of his Cistercian monastic life he had recognized the prime importance of rediscovering and deepening one's knowledge of the great spiritual tradition of Cîteaux, which belonged to everyone and was not the property of anyone in particular.

A man of prayer, he realized how important the liturgy is for the quality of monastic community life. So it was that from the beginning of his abbacy—and even before, when he was novice master—he devoted a great deal of his time and energy to composing a commentary on the liturgical year. The preponderant role he played in the Liturgy Commission of the Order, often preventing it from falling into preoccupation with rubrics or archaeology, is well known.

A practical and realistic man, he understood the importance of a firm canonical tradition which defines the rights and duties of each monk, spelling out the extent and limits of authority as well as the responsibilities of all those who have some duties to fulfill. Because of his clear mind, from the beginning of his abbacy he was called upon to work with the Commission in charge of revising the Constitutions after the publication of the Code of Canon Law. His successor, Dom Guerric Baudet, had the same role at the General Chapters after Vatican II. With Dom Anselme and after him, several monks of Scourmont—for example, Fr. Joseph Canivez and Fr. Colomban Bock—had a deep influence on canonical studies in the Order.

Nor did he forget that the tradition of the Order was expressed also in its architecture and in the administration of the monastery's patrimony. So it was quite natural that Dom Anselme Dimier, who had first been a monk of Tamié, came to pursue his brilliant career of research and writing at Scourmont. Dom Anselme's spirituality did not get lost in various particular devotions, as was often the case at that time. It was rooted in solid spiritual and mystical theology, and nourished by prolonged study in depth of the Rule of Saint Benedict and the Cistercian Fathers. One could say that, long before the expression was in vogue, he re-introduced *lectio divina* in the Order. From 1924 on he was thinking of a *Literary History of the Order of Cîteaux*, something like the *Histoire littéraire du sentiment religieux* by Henri Brémond, and in the line of the *Histoire littéraire du monachisme* which Dom Adalbert de Vogüé undertook.

Although the sum of what he wrote is enormous—especially his writings in preparation for his teaching to his community—he published very little. A whole generation of Scourmont monks formed in his school, however, deeply influenced the spiritual and intellectual life of the Order during the decades which preceded and followed the Second World War. In addition to those already mentioned, it suffices to mention Godefroid Bélorgey (loaned to Cîteaux for twenty years), Charles Dumont, Albert Derzelle, Camille Hontoir, Corneille Haflants, Maur Standaert, and a number of others. It was only at the time when most of these monks were quite advanced in their monastic life and in their careers as writers that the Order as a whole opened up little by little, during the years preceding the Council, to the importance of solid intellectual formation.

After the Council, however, the Order entered into a period of profound transformation. On the one hand, new foundations have not ceased to multiply in the Young Churches—Africa first of all, then Latin America and Asia; on the other hand, the number of vocations has diminished radically in communities of Europe and America.

Even if the Order continues to invest a great deal of effort in the formation of young monks and nuns, the lack of personnel in aging communities and the urgent needs of new foundations have had as a result that very little preoccupation has been given during the last twenty-five years to form real specialists in the fields dear to Dom Anselme: knowledge of the Cistercian Fathers, Liturgy, Law, Architecture, History. There are, no doubt, a great many excellent lay specialists in each one of these fields, and most of them are very sensitive to our type of life and have great respect for our values. But dialogue between lay scholars and monk and nun scholars of the same scientific calibre remains essential. This dialogue risks disappearing. If only for this reason, Dom Anselme's message is very meaningful and contemporary.

Still, Dom Anselme was above all a "father" who assured the growth of a community of free and adult monks who rendered quite naturally to their brothers and to the whole Order the services for which they had had the opportunity to be prepared. In our time, when theories on various types of "spiritual paternity" and various experiences of "new" and "old" community life draw monks and nuns in various directions, the message of Dom Anselme is a beam of light that is sure. This message invites us to center our formation on the Word of God and on an ever-renewed knowledge of the Cistercian tradition, as well as on knowledge of theology in general. That is how the "refoundation"—which the Order, like every religious institute, is called upon to accomplish periodically—can be brought about.

The fact that the present volume discreetly mentions *Cahiers Scourmontois* implies that other books will follow. This expresses the intention of the community of Scourmont to pursue, even though in a humble and limited way, its service to the Cistercian Order and to the whole *Ordo monasticus*, following the line traced by its illustrious abbot of yore. It is thus that it intends, not without a smile, to continue to give birth in its old age, like Sarah, opening wide the doors of her tent to the Three Visitors.

Dom Armand Veilleux
Abbot of Scourmont

Bibliography

(in chronological order)

La Règle de saint Benoît. Manuel de vie spirituelle, in *Compte-rendu de la retraite des Supérieurs à Cîteaux,* Westmalle, 1914, pp. 16–42.

Formation du moine à la liturgie, in *Compte-rendu, art. cit.,* pp. 92–115.

Les Trappistines, Scourmont, 1924. Booklet in—12, 16 pages.

Mémoire sur la publication d'une Collection cistercienne, 1925, 10 pages.

La spiritualité cistercienne, in *Les cahiers du cercle thomiste féminin,* 1927, pp. 388–413; 463–491.

L'influence de saint Bernard sur les auteurs spirituels de son temps, in *Saint Bernard et son temps,* t. I, Dijon, 1929, pp. 205–215.

La Règle de saint Benoît dans l'Ordre de Cîteaux, in *Revue liturgique et monastique,* Maredsous, 1929, pp. 134–154.

Saint Bernard, docteur de la vie liturgique, in *Revue liturgique et monastique,* Maredsous, 1930, pp. 26–35.

Saint Bernard, docteur de la dévotion à Notre Seigneur Jésus Christ, Gembloux, 1931, brochure in-12, 53 pages.

Note sur l'excommunication dans l'Ordre de Cîteaux, Scourmont, 1934.

Ordo commendationis animae, in *Actes de la Commission de liturgie,* Westmalle, 1937, pp. 1–3.

Benedictionale ad usum monachorum, in *Actes, art. cit.,* pp. 15–27.

Cérémonial de la manière de recevoir les Sœurs, Westmalle, 1937.

Coeremoniale Abbatum, Westmalle, 1939.

L'Ordre de Cîteaux. La Trappe, Paris, Letouzey, 1924; 17th edition, 1947.

Les exercices spirituels de saint Benoît dans l'Ordre de Cîteaux, in *Revue d'Ascétique et de Mystique, Mélanges Marcel Viller,* Toulouse, 1949, pp. 164–173.

Collaboration with the *Dictionnaire de Spiritualité*:

Adam de Perseigne, t. I, col. 198–201.

Aelred de Rievaulx, t. I, col. 225–234.

Bernard de Clairvaux, t. I, col. 1454–1499.

Collaboration with *Collectanea*:

La bibliographie de saint Etienne Harding, t. I, 1934, pp. 56–64.

La célébration du VIIIe centenaire de la mort de saint Etienne Harding, t. I, 1934, pp. 154–158.

Introduction au VIIIe centenaire de la mort de saint Bernard, t. VIII, 1946, pp. 91–97.

La paternité de saint Benoît dans l'Ordre de Cîteaux, t. IX, 1947, pp. 110–130.